Dyn

Conspiracies
Murders
Religion

by
Claudio Bocchia

This book tries to find a logical path to the events that ended the 18th Egyptian dynasty.

I don't claim to have the truth or to be an archaeologist, but I simply used my analytical mind to imagine a logical sequence of events that took place in the 14th century BC.

My passion for Egyptian history led to these writings.

INTRODUCTION

Thanks for joining me on this adventure in search of a plausible logic.

The end of the 18th dynasty is full of mysteries. 3500 years later, the time has come to imagine a logical sequel that ended this fascinating period of history.

The pharaohs such as Amenhotep III, Akhenaten, Tutankhamun, Ay, and Horemheb have left an indelible mark in history. But what really happened? The goal of every Egyptian was to reach eternal life, but the irony is that the young pharaoh Tutankhamun, whose reign was deliberately erased, became the most famous pharaoh in the world. To reach eternal life, the name of the pharaoh must be repeated over and over again, and it is clear that this goal was achieved for him.

This book tries to answer some questions that have remained unanswered until today. How did Tutankhamun die? Who succeeded Akhenaten? Who is Moses? How to interpret the mysteries surrounding the funeral rite of Tutankhamun? Who introduced the monotheistic religions that we know today?

My passionate gaze on Egyptian history allowed me to establish a theory that I share in this book. After watching hundreds of hours of reports and documentaries on the latest discoveries and hypotheses, I wondered if the use of my logical mind, usually employed in my professional life to design simple concepts and solutions to complex problems, could lead to a credible theory.

After reading this book, and the journey you will have taken in my company, you may have in your mind an alternative and answers to some of these questions.

Dear Reader, thank you for keeping this theory secret and for not sharing these hypotheses which, without a doubt, will debate within the scientific community.

In short, you want to know more? So don't wait any longer and join me in my theory.

CHAPTER I. THE TRAGIC FATE OF THE YOUNG PHARAOH

A TERRIBLE NEWS IS SPREADING

A piercing cry shatters the morning tranquility of the palace: "The king is dead! Our beloved pharaoh is no more!" The voice of a servant, trembling with emotion, carries the news that seems too cruel to be true.

The news, like a devastating wave, spreads through the corridors and rooms of the Pharaoh's palace. This imposing citadel of marble and granite, stands with undisputed majesty in the heart of Thebes, the resplendent capital of Egypt's 18th dynasty. The palace, more than a simple royal residence, is the symbol of the Pharaoh's divine power, the all-powerful sovereign of this prosperous and extended empire. It is also the nerve center of power and administration, where crucial decisions for the empire are made and where destinies are shaped.

In this architectural labyrinth, the rooms and courtyards are adorned with sumptuous frescoes and epic sculptures, telling the exploits of the gods and the pharaohs. The thick walls and massive columns, painted with bright colors and mythological scenes, rise to the sky, testifying to the power and glory of the Egyptian Empire. The luxurious rooms, bathed in light and perfumed with incense, myrrh and lotus flowers, welcome the pharaoh and his court. The reception and work rooms, filled with scribes and advisers, buzz with activity and plots. The fortified walls, guarded by imposing soldiers, ensure the safety of the pharaoh and his family.

But beyond its grandeur, the palace is a sanctuary of beauty and serenity. Its lush gardens, dotted with shimmering pools and divine statues, offer a haven of peace in the

midst of the city of Thebes' tumult. This thriving metropolis, located on the banks of the great Nile River, is a crossroads of cultures and power. Its busy streets, filled with merchants, artisans, and travelers, reflect the diversity and wealth of the empire. The majestic temples, dedicated to the gods and goddesses, dominate the urban landscape, while the schools and libraries attract scholars and students from all over the kingdom.

The rumor of the death of young king Tutankhamun, which occurred in the tenth year of his reign at the age of 19, spreads like a shock wave across the city and all the kingdom. The suddenness of his death leaves the people stunned and deeply saddened. His royal wife, Ankhesenamun, is overwhelmed by an abyssal sadness, her world collapsing around her.

At the palace, under the direction of Ay, the vizier, the preparations for the royal funeral begin with solemn urgency. The body of the young pharaoh lies on a funeral bed, his head delicately resting on a richly decorated headrest. Around him, counselors Ay and Horemheb, as well as his closest and most faithful servants, stand in respectful silence. Ankhesenamun, her eyes blurred with tears, stands by his side, gently stroking his cold hand.

A procession of high priests, governors, dignitaries, counselors, and nobles forms, each coming to pay their last respects to the young king. Tutankhamun is dressed in his fine linen loincloth, his chest covered in a gleaming gold breastplate, inlaid with lapis lazuli, silver, turquoise, and adorned with a scarab beetle pushing a solar disc of carnelian.

At nightfall, an unsettling atmosphere envelops the palace. The only sound is the crackling of torches, as servants keep watch over the royal body. The royal line of the 18th dynasty, now without a direct heir, is on the brink of collapse, threatening to plunge the empire into an era of uncertainty and chaos.

The streets of Thebes, once filled with singing and laughter, are now filled with a heavy silence. Merchants close their stalls earlier, priests in temples pray with renewed fervor, and citizens whisper with concern about the fate of their beloved empire. The sudden disappearance of their young king, a symbol of renewal and hope, leaves a huge void in the heart of each one.

In the days following, the city prepares for the royal funeral. Artisans and workers hurry to prepare the sarcophagus and tomb, while priests recite incantations to ensure the Pharaoh's safe passage into the afterlife. The streets fill with funeral processions, musicians playing melancholy melodies, and dancers performing sacred rituals to honor the deceased king.

The death of Tutankhamun is not only the end of a reign, but also the beginning of a period of great change and uncertainty. In the corridors of power, intrigues and plots multiply, each seeking to take advantage of the void left by the disappearance of the young pharaoh. The questions arise: who will take the crown? What will be the fate of the empire? And what revelations do the gods reserve for the future of Egypt?

The Purification in the Ibw

In the heart of ancient Thebes, three days after the unexpected death of the young pharaoh Tutankhamun, a solemn atmosphere enveloped the ibw, a temporary structure dedicated to ritual purification. In this sacred space, away from the noise of the world of the living, the body of the deceased king was to be prepared for his final odyssey to immortality.

At dawn, as the first rays of the Egyptian sun pierced the veil of night, the embalmers, dressed in immaculate linen, welcomed the body of Tutankhamun. Their task was sacred: to purify the young fallen sovereign for his journey into the afterlife. The body, once vibrant with youth and power, now lay inert, wrapped in eternal silence.

The expert embalmers' hands were busy with religious devotion. They delicately cleaned the body with water from the Nile, each drop of which was charged with mysticism and life. This water, the very essence of Egypt, symbolized purification and renewal, essential for the pharaoh's passage into the world of the gods.

After the body was washed, it was anointed with oils and precious essences. These substances, chosen for their preservative properties and their intoxicating aromas, were applied with ritual precision. The embalmers, in a silent ballet, gently massaged the skin of the pharaoh, perfuming it, preparing it to face eternity. Each touch was a goodbye, each anointing a prayer for his soul.

Around the body, the priests chanted ancient incantations, their voices rising and intertwining in a melodious chant that seemed to defy time. These formulas, passed down for generations, invoked the protection of the gods and guided the spirit of Tutankhamun through the dangers of the afterlife. The words, charged with power and faith, floated in the air, enveloping the body in a cocoon of the sacred.

After the purification ceremony in the ibw, the body of Tutankhamun began its solemn journey to the wabet, the sanctuary where the transformation into a mummy would take place. This passage, far from being simply a physical displacement, was loaded with symbolism and marked a crucial transition of the pharaoh's soul to immortality.

At dusk, as the sky took on shades of purple and gold, a silent and respectful procession formed. The embalmers, accompanied by priests and bearers, carried the body on an ornate litter, slowly crossing the sandy paths of Thebes. The cortege moved to the beat of drums and melancholy chants, creating an atmosphere of mystery and reverence.

The path to the wabet was a journey between two worlds: the world of the living and the world of the dead. Each step seemed to gradually erase the boundary between earthly reality and the spiritual realm. The spectators, witnesses of this sacred march, observed in silence, some with a heavy heart, others with deep veneration. The passage of the Pharaoh was a reminder of the fragility of life and the power of the afterlife.

Throughout the journey, offerings were placed on the altar of the gods, asking for their protection and goodwill for the king's soul's journey. The priests sprinkled the path with incense and flower petals, purifying the air and invoking the presence of the deities. These rituals, carried out with unshakeable precision and fervor, were essential to ensure a safe and sanctified passage for Tutankhamun into the afterlife.

Upon arrival at the wabet, a temporary but majestic structure, the body was greeted by a new team of specialized priests and embalmers. The wabet, bathed in the flickering light of torches, looked like a gateway between worlds, a place where the physical and metaphysical met. Here, the body would be subjected to the ancient art of mummification, a meticulous process that ensured that the king could live forever among the gods.

As the sun disappeared on the horizon, giving way to a starry sky, the body of Tutankhamun was delicately placed inside the wabet. This moment marked a final goodbye to the earthly world. The doors of the sanctuary slowly closed, enveloping the pharaoh in a peaceful darkness, a prelude to his rebirth in eternity.

The Mummification in the Wabet

In the sacred sanctuary of the wabet, the body of Tutankhamun entered the most crucial phase of its posthumous journey: mummification. This process, both artistic and spiritual, was carried out with extreme precision and care, transforming the mortal body of the young pharaoh into an eternal dwelling for his soul.

The embalmers, undisputed masters of their art, approached the body with a mixture of respect and solemnity. Their task was not only to preserve the body, but also to prepare it for its journey to the afterlife. Each gesture, each incision was imbued with deep ritual significance, transforming the wabet's chamber into a workshop where art and religion harmoniously merged.

The process began with the delicate removal of the internal organs. This step, far from being a simple medical procedure, was laden with symbolism. The organs were carefully extracted, with the exception of the heart, seat of thought and emotion, which was to remain in the body. Each organ was then treated, mummified and placed in canopic jars, silent guardians of the pharaoh's life essence.

The extraction of the brain, carried out with a long, thin hook, was an act of strange beauty. The ancient Egyptians did not accord it the same importance as the heart, but its manipulation remained a profound act of transformation. The brain was removed with care, liquefied and eliminated, leaving the head, seat of royalty, ready to be preserved for eternity.

Dehydration and Ointment

In the mysterious atmosphere of the wabet, the body of Tutankhamun underwent a remarkable transformation. After the organs were removed and the brain was removed, the body entered a crucial phase: dehydration and anointing. These steps, much more than simple physical procedures, were acts loaded with symbolism, essential to the preparation of the young king for his journey to the afterlife.

Dehydration began with the meticulous application of natron, an alkaline salt extracted from the salty lakes of Egypt. This compound, used for generations by embalmers, played a crucial role in the preservation of the body. For forty days and forty nights, the body rested, wrapped in this sacred salt, gradually losing all trace of moisture. Natron, acting as a bridge between the material world and the spiritual kingdom, purified the body, preparing it to become a receptacle for the pharaoh's eternal soul.

After the dehydration process, the body was carefully washed to remove any residue of natron, and then it was time for the anointing. The embalmers, like priests during a sacred ritual, would cover the body in oils and aromatic resins. These substances, chosen for their preserving properties and their links to the divine, would soak into the skin, making it soft and resistant. Cedar oil, myrrh, and other precious essences were applied in an order and manner that followed ancient traditions, transforming the body into a sacred work of art.

Each oil and resin used in the ointment had its own meaning. They were not only chosen for their physical qualities, but also for their spiritual associations. Cedar oil, for example, was reputed to repel evil spirits, while myrrh was considered a link to the divine world. The ointment was therefore an act of protection and sanctification, ensuring that the pharaoh's body would be both preserved from earthly dangers and blessed by the gods.

With the end of the anointing, Tutankhamun's body was ready for the final step of mummification: the bandaging. The body, now rigid and perfumed, was wrapped in linen bandages, marking the end of its transformation from mortal to deity. Each bandage, impregnated with magical formulas and prayers, added an additional layer of protection, sealing the pharaoh in a state of eternal preservation.

The Preparation of the Tomb

While embalmers were busy around the body of Tutankhamun, another group of artisans, just as dedicated, worked in the shadow of the Valley of the Kings. Their task: to prepare the young pharaoh's final tomb, an eternal sanctuary for his journey into the afterlife. This work, carried out under the careful supervision of Ay, the vizier and advisor to the king, was fraught with urgency and of paramount importance.

Ay chose a different tomb than the one originally planned for Tutankhamun. This choice, perhaps dictated by the premature and unexpected death of the Pharaoh, added additional pressure on the shoulders of the artisans. They had to quickly decorate the walls of the tomb, while respecting the rites and traditions that guided their hand.

The walls of the tomb were covered in detailed frescoes, illustrating scenes of everyday life, religious rituals, and representations of Tutankhamun with the deities. These images, painted with bright colors and minute details, were not simply decorations. They were powerful symbols, guides for the pharaoh in the afterlife, ensuring his protection and orientation in the world of the dead.

The hieroglyphs that adorned the walls were just as important. Each symbol, each line, was a magical formula, a message to the gods, or essential information about the life and death of the pharaoh. These texts, carefully engraved, were incantations intended to protect the king, guide him, and ensure his resurrection and eternal life.

The Valley of the Kings, with its red-hued mountains and arid hills, offered a majestic and mysterious setting for the final resting place of Tutankhamun. Each tomb, carved into the rock, was a world unto itself, a door between the world of the living and that of the gods. Tutankhamun's tomb, though smaller than those of some of his predecessors, was a masterpiece of art and architecture, a testament to the ingenuity and faith of the ancient Egyptians.

Under the pressure of time, the artisans worked day and night. The paint, often applied to still wet plaster, showed the haste with which the work was done. This haste, although necessary, had its consequences: mold appeared quickly after the tomb was closed, and some details of the frescoes and decorations were less refined than in other royal tombs. In addition, a chemical reaction between linseed oil and bandages caused the mummy to self-combust a few hours after the tomb was closed.

The Treasures of the Tomb

In the silent depths of the Valley of the Kings, the tomb of Tutankhamun, once sealed, became a hidden treasure, a time capsule of Egyptian greatness. Inside, in eternal darkness, lay unimaginable wealth, objects of extraordinary beauty and complexity, all intended to accompany the young pharaoh on his eternal journey.

The funeral mask of Tutankhamun, a jewel of goldsmithing, shone with a golden brilliance, forever capturing the young and serene features of the pharaoh. Inlaid with precious stones and lapis lazuli, the mask was a symbol of divine power, a bridge between man and the gods. The eyes, made of alabaster and enamel, seemed to look through time, testifying to a life once lived and an eternity promised.

The tomb was overflowing with various objects: sparkling jewelry, canopic vases to shelter the internal organs, statues of protective deities, and even a golden wooden funeral chariot. Each object had its place and its role, some for the king's daily life in the afterlife, others to ensure his protection and divine status.

Among the treasures, the ouchebtis held a special place. These small figurines, servants of the afterlife, were there to work in the place of the pharaoh in the world of the dead. Each ouchebti, with its appearance of a servant, was a promise of rest and freedom for Tutankhamun in his post-mortem existence.

The everyday objects, such as the gilded wooden furniture, the alabaster vases, and the jewelry, told the story of a royal life, full of pomp and ceremony. These treasures, beyond their material value, were symbols of the continuity of life, of the belief in an existence beyond death.

Each artifact, from games to musical instruments, from weapons to toiletries, was imbued with magic and intention. They were not simply material possessions, but essential components of a larger ritual, the rebirth and immortality of the king.

The Ouchebtis and Life After Death

In the heart of the eternal darkness of Tutankhamun's tomb, among the sparkling treasures and sacred relics, were the shabtis, silent witnesses of the Egyptian belief in life after death. These small figurines, shaped with care and devotion, were much more than simple works of art; they embodied the very essence of eternal life according to the ancient Egyptians.

In the tomb of Tutankhamun, the shabtis were arranged in orderly rows, like a small army ready to serve. Each figurine, with its painted face and individualized features, seemed ready to come to life and be active at the call of its master. This army was a guarantee against loneliness and inaction, an eternal companion for the young king in his silent kingdom.

The ouchebtis, beyond their ritual function, were also works of art, testifying to the skill and creativity of Egyptian artisans. Each figurine was unique, reflecting not only the status of the deceased, but also the art and culture of a civilization fascinated by the beyond.

Each ouchebti, carved in stone, wood, or clay, was designed to serve the pharaoh in the afterlife. These miniature servants, often shown with agricultural tools in their hands, were supposed to take on the deceased's arduous tasks in the realm of the dead. They symbolized the belief that even after death, earthly needs and daily obligations continued.

The ouchebtis were more than just a convenience; they were a link between the world of the living and the world of the gods. Each figurine was inscribed with a magical formula, often extracted from the Book of the Dead, ensuring that the ouchebti would rise and perform the required tasks. These incantations were a sacred pact, guaranteeing that the deceased would not be burdened by labor in his post-mortem existence.

The antechamber, the annex, the funeral room and the treasure room

At the bottom of Tutankhamun's tomb, beyond the narrow passages and secret chambers, were the antechamber and annex, spaces full of mystery and treasure. These rooms, though different in their function and content, together told a complex and fascinating story of life, death, and Egyptian belief in the afterlife. The treasure room contained the shrine of Anubis, the funerary god, as well as the canopic jars meant to hold the king's viscera.

The antechamber, the first room after the narrow passage, was a world where the temporal and the eternal met. The walls, whitewashed with lime and devoid of decorations, contrasted with the richness of the objects they housed. More than seven hundred pieces were crammed in there, creating a labyrinth of wealth and wonders.

Among these treasures, there were furniture made of gilded wood, ornate funeral beds, war and hunting chariots, and a multitude of the king's personal belongings. Each object told a story, a fragment of Tutankhamun's earthly life: weapons for the warrior, musical instruments for the art enthusiast, games for the player, and clothing for the elegant sovereign.

The annex, in comparison, seemed like a pantry for eternity. Here, in apparent disorder, were stored baskets, jars of wine, calcite dishes, and even boat models. This room served as a reserve for the afterlife, ensuring that the king would not lack anything in his eternal journey.

These two rooms, with their varied contents, offered a unique glimpse into everyday life in ancient Egypt. The antechamber, with its luxury items and furniture, reflected the royal status and grandeur of Tutankhamun, while the annex, with its provisions and utilitarian objects, reminded that even in death, earthly needs persisted.

The Precipitation and the Consequences

In the last days of the preparation of the tomb of Tutankhamun, a sense of urgency permeated the air. Ay, the vizier and co-regent, driven by unknown motives, pressed the artisans, embalmers and painters to finish their work with unusual speed. This haste, dictated by mysterious circumstances, would have lasting repercussions on the tomb and its occupant.

The embalming of Tutankhamun, normally a meticulous process spread over 70 days, was accelerated. The embalmers, working day and night, had to take shortcuts. The mummy of the young pharaoh, quickly wrapped in linen strips soaked in linseed oil, testified to this haste. This precipitousness led to an unexpected chemical reaction: self-combustion that blackened and degraded the mummy's skin, forever altering the young king's appearance in the afterlife.

The painters, too, worked against the clock. The frescoes, normally executed with care on dry walls, were painted on still-wet plaster. This method, although quick, had a cost: the quick appearance of mold on the walls, dulling the bright colors and the minute details of the scenes represented. The images of deities, rituals, and the everyday life of the Pharaoh, intended to guide and protect Tutankhamun in the afterlife, were thus compromised.

The precipitation also affected the quality and arrangement of the funeral objects. Precious artifacts, jewelry, statues, and furniture were placed in the tomb in an apparent disorder, reflecting the haste and perhaps even the dismay of the people charged with this sacred task. This chaotic disposition contrasted sharply with the order and symmetry usually observed in Egyptian royal tombs.

This haste, dictated by reasons still veiled in mystery, had consequences not only on the physical state of the tomb and the mummy, but also on the perception of Tutankhamun in history. The young king, destined to rest forever in splendor and respect, was thus wrapped in a veil of mystery and neglect.

The Seal of Destiny

As the final preparations for the tomb of Tutankhamun came to an end, a solemn silence enveloped the Valley of the Kings. The artisans, priests and workers had withdrawn, leaving behind the sealed tomb, an eternal sanctuary for the young pharaoh. This moment not only marked the end of a rushed funeral process but also the beginning of a mystery that would captivate the world for millennia.

The seal of Tutankhamun's tomb, a simple piece of stamped clay, symbolized much more than a physical closure. It was a seal of destiny, marking the pharaoh's transition from the world of the living to the world of the dead. This seal, applied with a last prayer and a breath of hope, was supposed to protect the king against intrusions and disturbances, preserving his journey into the afterlife.

Despite the intentions and rituals, Tutankhamun's rest was destined to be disturbed. The seal, which was supposed to remain unbroken until the end of time, was broken by the hands of tomb raiders, eager for treasure and insensitive to the curses and warnings of the ancients. Fortunately, an unexpected flood finally buried the tomb and preserved it from the tomb raiders of ancient times, the tomb of Tutankhamun escaped largely from this profanation, remaining relatively intact until its rediscovery in 1922 by Howard Carter.

The rediscovery of the tomb, with its broken seal, opened a new chapter in the history of Tutankhamun, revealing to the world the wealth and mysteries of ancient Egypt. The broken seal, once a symbol of protection and sanctity, became a symbol of curiosity and discovery, offering a rare and precious glimpse into the life of a forgotten Pharaoh.

The seal of Tutankhamun's destiny, although broken, continued to protect his legacy. The treasures, artifacts and knowledge revealed by the tomb opened a window on an ancient civilization, its beliefs, its arts and its ingenuity. Tutankhamun, during his lifetime a minor king, became in death an eternal symbol of ancient Egypt, his golden face and his funeral mask becoming world-renowned icons.

CHAPTER II. THE WORLD OF AMENHOTEP

THE YOUNG PRINCE

Childhood and Education

But let's go back a few decades to the time of Amenhotep III (future father of Akhenaten and grandfather of Tutankhamun). In the vast and opulent halls of the royal palace of Egypt, where the scents of incense mixed with the gentle fragrances of the blue lotus, the young prince Amenhotep III was growing up. The walls, adorned with frescoes in bright colors, told stories of gods and pharaohs, while the columns of granite, tall and majestic, seemed to watch over him. The young prince, whose eyes sparkled with an insatiable curiosity, strode through the corridors, amazed by the splendor that surrounded him.

Every day, under the deep blue sky of Egypt, Amenhotep III received a royal education. His tutors, wise and learned men, taught him the art of calligraphy, the mastery of ancient languages, and the secrets of Egyptian history. In the gardens of the palace, where the air was always fresh and scented with jasmine and roses, he learned poetry and music, captivating his audience with his melodious voice and his skill in playing the golden lyre.

Learning diplomacy and war

But Amenhotep III's life was not only made of luxury and leisure. His mother Moutemouia as well as his father, the Pharaoh Thutmose IV, a man as wise as he was powerful, made sure that the young prince was also trained in the art of diplomacy and war strategies. In the council rooms, decorated with scenes of battles and hunts, Amenhotep III attentively observed the nobles and generals discuss the state's affairs. He learned to decipher the subtleties of political language, to understand the stakes of power, and to anticipate the movements of enemies.

During the rare moments of respite, the prince retreated to the hanging gardens of the palace, where the air was saturated with the intoxicating scents of orange blossoms. He contemplated the reflections of the sun on the Nile, thoughtful, dreaming of the days when he would lead his people into an era of prosperity and glory.

In the arena of the palace, under the severe but benevolent gaze of his father, Amenhotep III was practicing combat. The clinking of swords and the dull sound of shields echoed in the hot, dry air. Sweat beaded on his forehead as he wielded the sword with skill that even the most seasoned warriors were impressed by. He was learning not only to fight, but also to respect his adversary, to understand the importance of strength and wisdom.

The young prince grew up within the walls of his ancestral palace, preparing to become Amenhotep III, one of the greatest pharaohs of ancient Egypt. His childhood was a mixture of gilded dreams and earthly realities, a prelude to a reign that would be both a testament to the greatness of Egypt and a reflection of his own glory.

Political studies and preparations

As Amenhotep III approached adulthood, preparations for his future reign intensified. The secret chambers of the palace, where rays of sunlight filtered through finely woven linen curtains, became the stage for his intensive studies. Surrounded by stacks of papyrus and leather scrolls, the prince immersed himself in ancient texts, absorbing the teachings of the great pharaohs who came before him. He studied laws, treaties, and military strategies, his mind sharpened like a blade, ready to carve out the future of his kingdom.

In these rooms, where the air was always filled with the smell of wax and ink, Amenhotep III learned to govern. He became familiar with the complexities of administering an empire, the nuances of taxation, the importance of justice, and the delicate balance between tradition and innovation. Detailed maps of Egypt and its neighboring territories covered the walls, and the prince spent hours studying them, tracing the trade routes, borders, and strategic sites with his finger.

Intrigues at Court

But the most valuable lessons often came from within the palace walls, where intrigues were woven like spider webs in the dark corners. Amenhotep III, with a maturity that surpassed his young age, learned to navigate these murky waters. He observed, listened, and learned. The whispers of the courtiers, the muffled laughter behind the fans of ibis feathers, and the exchanged looks under the hieroglyphic pillars revealed the hidden alliances, the secret ambitions, and the concealed jealousies.

The young prince learned to discern the truth behind the masks of courtesy, to understand that every favor asked had a price, that every promise made was a thread in the great fabric of power. He learned to be suspicious and to trust, to maneuver with caution in the labyrinth of ambitions and desires.

In the gardens of the palace, where the scents of myrrh and aloe mixed with the sweetness of the night air, Amenhotep III often meditated on the lessons of the day. The twinkling stars above him seemed to guide his thoughts, reminding him of the greatness of the universe and the modest, but significant, place he occupied in it.

These years of preparation not only forged Amenhotep III into a future pharaoh, but also a visionary leader, a skilled strategist, and a shrewd diplomat. He stood at the dawn of his reign, ready to embrace his destiny, to guide Egypt into an era of unparalleled splendor, driven by the dreams of glory and the realities of a world in constant change.

Infrastructure and expansion projects

In Amenhotep III's mind, the image of a vast and flourishing empire was taking shape, a grandiose vision that went far beyond the borders of Egypt. He dreamed of vast infrastructure projects, envisioning sparkling canals under the Egyptian sun, commercial routes extending like veins across the desert, and prosperous cities where trade and culture could flourish.

The halls of the palace echoed with animated discussion about these ambitious projects. Amenhotep III, surrounded by his architects and engineers, unrolled detailed plans, his fingers sliding over the lines that represented majestic temples, imposing dams, and sumptuous palaces. He imagined structures that would defy time, monuments that would speak of his greatness through the ages.

Dreams of grandeur for Egypt

But it was not only architectural grandeur that occupied Amenhotep III's thoughts. He dreamed of an Egypt where art, science, and philosophy would reach unprecedented heights. He envisioned libraries filled with knowledge, workshops of artisans where creativity would have no limits, and academies where the brightest minds could debate and learn.

In the luxurious gardens of the palace, where lotus flowers opened at the touch of dawn and where birds sang ancient melodies, Amenhotep III walked, lost in his thoughts. He imagined a transformed Egypt, an empire where peace and prosperity would reign, where distant peoples would come to seek wisdom and inspiration.

Amenhotep III's vision for his empire was tinted with bright colors and golden light. He saw colorful processions in the streets of Thebes, markets overflowing with exotic products, and festivals where music, dance, and poetry would celebrate life and the gods. Every stone laid, every column erected, every statue carved would be a testament to Egyptian greatness, a message of eternity engraved in stone and time.

Amenhotep III, with this vision in mind, was preparing to take the reins of power. He knew that the challenges would be many, but his determination was unshakeable. He stood on the threshold of a new era, ready to guide Egypt towards a radiant future, a future where his dreams of greatness would come true, leaving an indelible mark in the history of humanity.

AMENHOTEP III THE MAGNIFICENT

The Ascension to the Throne

The day of Amenhotep III's ascension to the throne of Egypt was marked by unparalleled splendor. The sky, a deep blue, seemed to open up to welcome the reign of the young pharaoh. The Nile, shimmering in the hot sun, reflected the colorful flags and sails of the decorated boats, while the banks echoed with the chants and cheers of the crowd.

The ceremonies began at dawn, with majestic processions winding through the streets of Thebes. Priests in ceremonial robes, carrying censers, led the way, followed by musicians whose lyres, drums, and flutes created an enchanting melody. Dancers and acrobats in dazzling costumes captivated the crowd with their graceful movements and daring feats.

In the heart of the procession, Amenhotep III, dressed in fine linen and sparkling jewelry, was carried by his servants on a golden palanquin. His gaze, both proud and serene, swept the multitude, while his people acclaimed him with fervor. The rays of the sun reflected on his diadem, surrounding him with an almost divine aura.

When the procession reached the great temple of Amun, a respectful silence fell over the crowd. Amenhotep III descended from his palanquin and climbed the steps of the temple, each step echoing the beginning of a new era. Inside, the walls covered in hieroglyphs and colorful frescoes testified to centuries of devotion and power.

The priests, in a sacred choreography, led Amenhotep III to the altar where the coronation rites were taking place. Incense, sacred chants and offerings to the gods were mixed in a mystical ballet, while the young pharaoh received the insignia of his power: the scepter and the crown, symbols of his sovereignty over the Two Lands.

At the end of the ceremony, Amenhotep III appeared on the balcony of the temple, facing his people. The sun, at its zenith, bathed the pharaoh in a golden light, accentuating the splendor of his attire and the brilliance of his gaze. He raised his arms, and an unanimous acclamation rose from the thousands of people gathered, saluting the beginning of a reign that promised greatness and prosperity.

At nightfall, Thebes was illuminated by a thousand fires. Banquets were organized, rare wines flowed in abundance, and laughter and animated conversations filled the air. The stars twinkled in the sky, silent witnesses to the dawn of a new era under the reign of Amenhotep III the Magnificent, a reign that would be written in the annals of history in letters of gold and glory.

A Reign of Splendor

The reign of Amenhotep III the Magnificent was marked by an unprecedented period of peace and prosperity. The Nile, this vital artery of Egypt, flowed peacefully, its waters nourishing the fertile lands and ensuring abundant harvests. The markets of Thebes were teeming with exotic products, testifying to the flourishing trade with distant lands.

The streets were alive with the sweet smell of spices, ripe fruits, and freshly picked flowers. The merchants, dressed in colorful tunics, proudly displayed their wares, while the musicians played enchanting melodies, adding to the festive atmosphere.

The granaries of Egypt were overflowing with grain, and the royal coffers were overflowing with gold and precious stones. The prosperity of the kingdom was palpable on every street corner, every smile on the faces of the inhabitants testifying to their happiness and pride.

The Temple of the Sun at Karnak, for example, was a wonder of engineering. Its massive columns, adorned with delicately carved hieroglyphs, rose towards the sky, creating an atmosphere of devotion and respect. The interior of the temple was a true masterpiece, with colorful frescoes depicting mythological scenes and royal exploits.

The artists, under the royal patronage, created works of unparalleled beauty and finesse. The sculptures, detailed and realistic, seemed to come to life under the skilled hands of the artisans. The paintings, with their bright colors and delicate patterns, captured the very essence of Egyptian splendor.

Each stone, each column, each fresco testified to the artistic vision of Amenhotep III and his desire to leave an indelible mark on the history of Egypt. His reign, characterized by artistic and architectural splendor, remains engraved in the annals as one of the most brilliant periods of ancient Egypt.

The palaces of Amenhotep III were masterpieces of architecture, adorned with vibrant frescoes and detailed sculptures. The royal gardens, with their rows of statues and basins reflecting the blue sky of Egypt, were meeting places for intellectuals and artists, where new ideas were discussed and works of art created.

In the royal workshops, the artists worked with precious materials, creating objects of breathtaking beauty intended to glorify the reign of Amenhotep III. The painters, with their fine brushes, captured the greatness of the empire and the majesty of the pharaoh, while the sculptors shaped the clay and stone to give life to divine and royal forms.

Amenhotep III himself was often seen touring these workshops, admiring the works in progress and offering words of encouragement. His passion for the arts and culture was not only a way to beautify his empire, but also to capture the essence of his time and leave a lasting legacy for future generations.

Under the reign of Amenhotep III, Egypt shone like a jewel of civilization, a place where wisdom, beauty, and culture were not only appreciated but also actively cultivated. His reign will remain in history as a golden age of prosperity, peace, and cultural splendor.

The Secrets of the Pharaoh

In the secret corridors of the palace of Amenhotep III, the air was charged with mystery and tension. The pharaoh, known for his wisdom and intelligence, was a master in the art of information management. He understood that knowledge was a powerful tool, especially when it came to thwarting conspiracies and maintaining order in his vast empire.

The secret rooms of the palace, lit by flickering oil lamps, were the scene of discreet meetings where Amenhotep III and his most loyal advisers exchanged information gathered by a network of spies. These spies, like shadows, roamed the empire, collecting whispers of rebellion, rumors of betrayal, and secrets of distant alliances.

Amenhotep III, seated on his ebony throne inlaid with gold and precious stones, listened attentively, his piercing eyes reflecting the light of the torches. He weighed each word, each piece of information, skillfully weaving his web to ensure the stability and security of his reign.

But Amenhotep III was not only a strategist and a keeper of secrets; he was also a fervent protector of the arts and culture. Under his reign, Egypt experienced a golden age of culture, where artists, poets, and musicians were cherished and encouraged.

Architectural Achievements

Under the azure sky of Egypt, the temples and palaces built by Amenhotep III rose, structures that defied time and space, embodying the divine and earthly greatness of the pharaoh. Every carved stone, every erected column told a story of power, devotion, and art.

The temples, with their vast courtyards open to the sky, their obelisks pointing to the heavens, and their mysterious sanctuaries plunged into semi-darkness, were places of worship and celebration. The walls were adorned with detailed bas-reliefs, depicting scenes of battles, religious rituals, and offerings to the gods. The bright colors of the frescoes contrasted with the gilded statues of the gods and the pharaoh, creating a dazzling visual spectacle.

The palaces of Amenhotep III, on the other hand, were wonders of architecture and luxury. Immense and majestic, they stood like fortresses of splendor in the midst of lush gardens and shimmering pools. The throne rooms, vast and airy, were sumptuously decorated, with painted ceilings of celestial motifs and walls inlaid with precious stones and dazzling mosaics.

Each temple and palace built by Amenhotep III was not only a work of architectural art, but also a symbol of his divine power. He firmly believed that his architectural achievements were a manifestation of his divine will and a way to get closer to the gods.

The temples were designed to reflect the cosmic order and divine majesty. The axes of the temples aligned with the stars and the solstices, creating a harmonious link between heaven and earth. The colossal statues of Amenhotep III, often placed at the entrance of the temples, represented the pharaoh as a living god, an intermediary between men and divinities.

In these sacred spaces, Amenhotep III organized grandiose ceremonies, where music, singing and dancing mixed with religious rituals, reinforcing his image of a Pharaoh-god. The processions, offerings and prayers in these temples and palaces were not only acts of devotion, but also demonstrations of the power and piety of Amenhotep III.

Thus, the architectural achievements of Amenhotep III were much more than simple stone structures; they were the beating heart of his empire, living symbols of his eternal reign, and testimony to the intimate relationship between the pharaoh, his people, and the gods.

A Reign of Peace and Prosperity

In Amenhotep III's Egypt, peace and stability reigned like silent guardians over a prosperous kingdom. The pharaoh, with his wisdom and foresight, had established a system of governance that ensured order and justice throughout the country. The laws were applied with equity, and the royal officials, chosen for their integrity and competence, ensured that every citizen was treated with respect and dignity.

The borders of Egypt were well guarded, not only by brave soldiers but also by strategic alliances and peace treaties. Amenhotep III, a master of diplomacy, had managed to maintain good relations with the neighboring kingdoms, thus avoiding unnecessary and costly conflicts. His governance was a skillful mix of force and flexibility, of tradition and innovation, thus ensuring the stability and longevity of his reign.

Libraries and schools multiplied, becoming centers of knowledge and wisdom. Scholars and scribes studied and preserved ancient knowledge while exploring new areas of knowledge. Science, medicine, astronomy, and literature developed, enriching the intellectual and cultural life of Egypt.

Thus, the reign of Amenhotep III was marked by lasting peace, wise governance, and prosperity that affected all aspects of Egyptian life. His reign was considered a golden age, a period when Egypt radiated power, wealth, and culture, an inheritance that would endure well beyond his time on earth.

THE HAREM OF AMENHOTEP III

Luxury and Sensuality

Amehotep III, also known as the pharaoh of a thousand wives, paid special attention to diplomacy through carnal alliances. The harem of Amenhotep III, nestled in the heart of majestic Thebes, was a world apart, a sanctuary of luxury and sensuality. It was a place where the opulence of the Egyptian empire was manifested in every detail: walls adorned with delicate frescoes, floors covered with soft and colorful carpets, and high ceilings supported by carved columns. The luxurious gardens of the harem, with their shimmering pools and flower-lined paths, offered a haven of freshness and beauty.

The harem served as a residence for the pharaoh's wives, concubines, and servants. It was both a private and sacred place, designed to ensure the comfort and well-being of its occupants. The rooms were spacious and richly decorated, furnished with comfortable beds, embroidered cushions, and light curtains that danced to the rhythm of the breeze.

The women of Amenhotep III's harem played various and vital roles. They were not only the pharaoh's companions; they were also mothers, advisers, and guardians of cultural and religious traditions. Each woman, whether she was the main wife, concubine, or servant, had her own story, her own role in the complex fabric of the royal court.

The primary wives, often from noble families or foreign royal lines, had a special status. They could influence political decisions and often had a say in state affairs. Their rooms, located near the pharaoh's, were spaces of power where alliances were formed and crucial decisions were made.

The concubines, chosen for their beauty and charm, brought joy and comfort to the pharaoh. They were also trained in the arts - dance, music, poetry - to entertain and charm not only the pharaoh but also the guests of honor.

The servants, meanwhile, ensured the proper functioning of the harem. They took care of everything, from preparing meals to maintaining the rooms, while keeping the secrets of the harem. Although their role was less glamorous, it was essential to the everyday life and luxury of the harem.

In this closed and protected world, the women of Amenhotep III's harem led a life that was both opulent and restricted, playing a crucial role in maintaining the tradition, culture, and politics of the Egyptian empire.

Politics and Power

Within Amenhotep III's harem, political intrigues and power games were not the exclusive domain of men. Women, particularly the chief wives and mothers of princes, exercised considerable influence, often underestimated, on the political decisions and strategic orientations of the kingdom. They were the confidantes, advisers, and sometimes even the emissaries of the Pharaoh, playing a key role in diplomacy and governance.

These women, endowed with a sharp intelligence and a deep understanding of state affairs, used their position to shape policies and alliances. In the luxurious salons and secret gardens of the harem, they wove networks of influence, exchanging information, negotiating support, and consolidating their power. Their influence often extended far beyond the walls of the palace, impacting international relations and the internal stability of Egypt.

Diplomatic marriages were a common and strategic practice in ancient Egypt, used by Amenhotep III to forge and strengthen alliances with other powers. Foreign princesses, integrated into the royal harem, became pawns in the great game of diplomacy. These marriages were not just personal unions but political acts, symbolizing peace, friendship, and sometimes the submission of foreign nations.

These foreign wives, often accompanied by their own court and customs, brought with them a wealth of culture and politics. They could serve as channels of communication with their countries of origin, influencing international relations and foreign policy. Their presence in the harem was a constant reminder of the links and commitments made by Amenhotep III to other kingdoms.

These marriages were also an opportunity for the pharaoh to demonstrate his magnanimity and his power. The wedding ceremonies, lavish and sumptuous, were state events, celebrating not only the union of two people but also the union of two nations. The festivities could last for several days, with processions, banquets and shows, reflecting the greatness and wealth of the Egyptian empire.

Through these unions, Amenhotep III's harem became a microcosm of the empire itself, a place where different cultures, languages, and political influences mixed. The women of the harem, whether Egyptian or foreign, played a crucial role in the complex web of diplomacy and power, helping to shape the history and destiny of ancient Egypt.

THE SED PARTY

Celebration and Significance

The Sed Festival, an event of paramount importance in ancient Egypt, was a grandiose celebration marking the thirty years of reign of Amenhotep III. This celebration, beyond its festive aspect, was a ritual of regeneration and renewal of the strength and legitimacy of the pharaoh. It took place in a sumptuous setting, within the majestic temples and on the vast public squares, transformed for the occasion into scenes of festivities.

The preparations for the SED Festival were a spectacle in themselves, involving months of planning and the mobilization of thousands of people. Artisans, priests, musicians, dancers, and workers were busy creating a setting worthy of this event. Statues and obelisks were erected, mythological scenes were painted and carved, and altars were set up for offerings to the gods.

On the day of the festival, Amenhotep III appeared in all his splendor, wearing ceremonial clothing adorned with precious stones and sacred symbols. He was accompanied by solemn processions, priests singing hymns, and the Egyptian nobility in full dress. The population, gathered in large numbers, watched demonstrations of force, ritual races, and reenactments of battles, symbolizing the pharaoh's renewed power and endurance.

The SED festival was laden with symbolism. It represented not only the physical and spiritual regeneration of the Pharaoh but also the reaffirmation of his divine power over Egypt. By presenting himself as a renewed and invincible sovereign, Amenhotep III strengthened his image as an undisputed leader and semi-god in the eyes of his people and his enemies.

Politically, the Sed Festival served to consolidate the authority of the Pharaoh. It was a demonstration of the stability and continuity of the reign, a clear message addressed to both internal dignitaries and foreign kingdoms. Alliances were strengthened, vassals reassured, and the ambitions of rivals discouraged.

In short, the Sed Festival of Amenhotep III was much more than a simple celebration; it was an event with profound repercussions, a dazzling mix of ritual, religion, politics and spectacle, reflecting the complexity and greatness of ancient Egypt.

Amenhotep III, Living God

The proclamation of Amenhotep III as a living god was a moment of transcendent importance, marking a turning point in the religious and political history of ancient Egypt. This declaration was not only an act of faith, but also a demonstration of absolute power, merging the earthly and celestial authority into one figure.

The ceremonies surrounding this proclamation were sumptuous and steeped in the sacred. They took place in great temples, like those of Karnak and Thebes, where priests, nobles, and citizens gathered in great numbers. Amenhotep III, dressed in ceremonial clothing adorned with divine symbols and crowned with the solar disk, presented himself to the crowd, surrounded by singing, incense, and the resonance of sistrums and drums.

The priests officiated complex rituals, invoking the gods and binding the Pharaoh to the divine. Hymns were sung in honor of Amenhotep III, now considered the earthly incarnation of a god, an intermediary between the world of men and that of the gods. This proclamation was also an opportunity to strengthen the ties between the Pharaoh and the clergy, affirming his role as protector and patron of temples and religious practices.

The descent of the Nile and demonstration of divinity

The descent of the Nile by Amenhotep III, in response to his proclamation as a living god, was a spectacular event, laden with symbolism and majesty. The pharaoh, on a large royal boat, descended the sacred river, showing himself to his people as a god. The boat, sumptuously decorated with gold and precious stones, reflected the rays of the sun, creating an almost supernatural aura around the sovereign.

This descent was not only a demonstration of power and divinity, but also an act of communion with the Egyptian people. The banks of the Nile came alive with crowds come to catch a glimpse of their Pharaoh-god, offering prayers and songs in his honor. Stops were made in major cities, where Amenhotep III participated in ceremonies and made offerings to local temples, thus reinforcing his image as a pious and benevolent ruler.

The descent of the Nile was also an act of renewal and purification, symbolizing the eternal link between the pharaoh, the nourishing river, and the cycle of life and rebirth. It was a living affirmation of the cosmic order, with Amenhotep III at the center, ensuring the continuity and stability of the universe.

In short, Amenhotep III's proclamation as a living god and his descent down the Nile were immense events, reflecting the unique fusion of religion, politics, and culture in ancient Egypt. These acts not only strengthened Amenhotep III's divine status but also his inseparable connection with his people and his country.

Majestic Funeral

The funeral of Amenhotep III was an event of unparalleled grandeur and solemnity, marking the end of a reign that had shaped Egypt into an unprecedented power. The disappearance of the Pharaoh was felt as a great loss throughout the kingdom, and the preparations for his funeral reflected this deep sadness mixed with sacred respect.

The ceremonies began with grandiose processions, where the pharaoh's body, placed in a massive gold sarcophagus, was transported on a chariot pulled by majestic horses. The priests in ceremonial robes, the nobles, the courtiers, and the ordinary citizens followed in a silent cortege, their funeral chants rising into the air as a poignant farewell to the deceased sovereign.

The rituals were accompanied by the offering of incense, food, and precious goods, intended to accompany Amenhotep III into the afterlife. Sacred texts were recited, invoking the protection of the gods and assuring the pharaoh a peaceful journey to the afterlife. The priests performed rites of purification and passage, symbolizing Amenhotep III's transition from the world of the living to the world of the gods.

The tomb of Amenhotep III, located in the Valley of the Kings, was an architectural wonder, designed to be an eternal palace for the pharaoh. Deeply carved into the rock, the tomb was adorned with detailed frescoes, hieroglyphs, and scenes depicting the pharaoh in various acts of divinity and power. The bright colors and complex patterns told the story of his life, his conquests, and his accomplishments.

Inside, Amenhotep III's sarcophagus was surrounded by priceless treasures: jewelry, statues, weapons, and ritual objects, all designed to serve the pharaoh in his afterlife. Magical amulettes and talismans were meticulously arranged around his corpse, offering protection and power in the realm of the dead.

The secret chambers of the tomb also housed a treasure trove of knowledge: papyrus containing religious texts, medical treatises, and travel stories, testifying to the intellectual and cultural richness of the time of Amenhotep III. These artifacts, discovered centuries later, offer a fascinating glimpse into life and death in ancient Egypt.

The funeral of Amenhotep III, with its majestic rituals and its sumptuous tomb, was a reflection of the greatness of a Pharaoh whose reign had marked a golden age for Egypt. These ceremonies, steeped in mysticism and splendor, have engraved in the memory of history the passage of a king who has become legend.

Heritage and Succession

The reign of Amenhotep III left an indelible mark on the history and culture of ancient Egypt. Amenhotep III was commemorated not only as a great builder, but also as a wise sovereign who had managed to maintain peace and promote the prosperity of his people. The temples, statues, and monuments he had erected remained as testimony to his greatness, and the stories of his exploits and wisdom were told from generation to generation.

The cultural impact of Amenhotep III was also profound. His patronage of the arts had led to a period of artistic renewal, where sculpture, painting, and architecture had reached new heights of expression and beauty. The artists and artisans, inspired by the vision and patronage of the pharaoh, had created works that continued to inspire and delight.

Tiyi: The Queen of the Shadow

Tiyi, wife of Amenhotep III and mother of Thutmose, Amenhotep IV(Akhenaten), Sitamun, Iset, Henuttaneb, Nebetah and Beketaten, remains one of the most powerful and enigmatic female figures of ancient Egypt. Her influence, extending well beyond the confines of the royal palace, shaped the history and politics of her time.

Tiyi was not of royal blood, but her marriage to Amenhotep III propelled her to the top of power. She quickly became more than just a wife: a counselor, a co-regent, and a political force in her own right. Her intelligence, wisdom, and charisma allowed her to skillfully navigate the murky waters of the court and Egyptian politics.

Tiyi played a crucial role in the promotion of arts and culture, influencing the construction of temples and the creation of art. She was also a central figure in the evolution of religious beliefs, actively participating in the development of the worship of Aten, which would later dominate under the reign of her son Akhenaten.

The life of Tiyi is surrounded by mysteries. Rumors about her origins, her religious beliefs, and even her role in court intrigues circulated abundantly. Some said she possessed occult knowledge, others that she was the true force behind the throne, guiding the decisions of her husband and son.

Despite the mysteries and speculation, Tiyi was deeply respected, both in Egypt and abroad. The kings of neighboring nations recognized her as a figure of power, addressing their correspondence to her directly, a rare mark of honor for a queen.

The legacy of Tiyi endures long after her death. The monuments and artworks she inspired continue to bear witness to her influence. Her tomb, rich in artifacts and symbols, provides a fascinating glimpse into her life and status.

The Builders of the Empire

Amenhotep III, nicknamed the "Magnificent", was a pharaoh builder. Under his reign, Egypt saw the erection of grandiose monuments, majestic temples and colossal statues. The temple of millions of years and the famous Colosses of Memnon, silent guardians of his funerary temple, still bear witness today to this architectural grandeur.

This was also a period of artistic revolution. Artists, under royal patronage, developed a more natural and detailed style, moving away from rigid previous conventions. The sculptures and paintings of this time reflect a finesse and attention to detail that were unprecedented, capturing life, nature, and divinity with a new grace and vibrancy.

Amenhotep III was a master of diplomacy. His reign was characterized by peaceful and fruitful relations with neighboring nations. Thanks to diplomatic marriages, trade agreements and peace treaties, he extended Egypt's influence well beyond its traditional borders, weaving a network of alliances that strengthened Egypt's position as a world power.

Although his reign was primarily peaceful, Amenhotep III did not neglect the art of war. He maintained and strengthened the Egyptian army, thus ensuring the security and stability of the empire. His military campaigns, although less frequent than those of his predecessors, were strategically targeted to consolidate and expand Egyptian territory.

The legacy of Amenhotep III continued long after his death. The monuments he built, the works of art he inspired, and the alliances he forged shaped the history of ancient Egypt. His reign, a harmonious mix of grandeur, art, and diplomacy, remains a golden chapter in the annals of the pharaohs.

Chapter III. Akhenaten, the Heretical Pharaoh

The Beginnings of a Royal Destiny

Akhenaten: The Awakening of a Prince

In the golden sands of ancient Egypt, under the benevolent gaze of an omnipresent sun, the young Akhenaten, born under the name of Amenhotep IV, opened his eyes to a world where the gods whispered in the wind and where the destiny of a man could shape the course of an empire. Son of the great Pharaoh Amenhotep III and the majestic Queen Tiyi, he was born in the purple, surrounded by riches and mysteries, destined to rule over the Two Lands.

His first steps were guided by the priests and the wise, who saw in him not only a future sovereign but the living incarnation of a deity. His education was as vast as the Nile, covering the art of war waged from glittering chariots, the subtle diplomacy that wove ties with distant kingdoms, and the deep knowledge of rituals that pleased the gods.

The palace of Thebes, with its grandiose colonnades and lush gardens, was his playground, and the temples, his classrooms. He learned to read the stars, to decipher the hieroglyphs that told the story of his ancestors, and to understand the complexities of administering a kingdom that extended far beyond the horizon.

But it was not only his intellect that was nurtured, his soul was also shaped by the mysteries of Egyptian faith. He stood alongside the priests in the darkened, incensed sanctuaries, learning the incantations and offerings that maintained cosmic order and ensured the prosperity of his people.

Akhenaten was growing up under the watchful eye of counselors and courtiers, but there was a spark of independence in him, a burning desire to leave his own mark on the sand of time. He dreamed of an empire where the sun would never set, an empire that would reflect the glory of the gods themselves.

And as the years passed, the young prince slowly transformed. He was no longer only the heir of Amenhotep III, he was becoming a force in himself, a mind that burned with a vision that would one day enlighten or consume Egypt. It was the awakening of a prince, the beginning of a story that would forever change the face of the ancient world.

In the cool shadow of the stone columns of the palace of Thebes, the young Akhenaten, heir to the pharaonic power, was immersed in the rigorous learning reserved for future rulers of Egypt. Surrounded by rolled papyrus and erudite scribes, he avidly drank knowledge like the Nile nourishes green fields.

Every day, he was initiated into the arcane of politics and strategy, learning to decipher the complexities of international relations and the subtleties of governance. The best teachers were at his disposal, teaching him not only to read and write, but also to understand the sacred responsibilities of his future role.

He studied the great texts of Egyptian wisdom, memorizing the maxims that would guide his decisions, and learned the laws that maintained order in an empire where the goddess of divine justice Maat , was the cornerstone of society. The priests of Amun, Ptah and Ra taught him the rites and prayers, revealing the secrets of the gods who watched over the kingdom of the living and the dead.

The path to the crown of Egypt was paved with imperative lessons and rites of passage that only a royal heir like Akhenaten could take. Each day that passed brought him closer to the moment when he would become the intermediary between the gods and men, the sovereign of the black and red earth, Egypt.

In the secret rooms of the palace, far from the eyes of the people, Akhenaten was initiated into the mysteries of the gods. The priests, guardians of the sacred knowledge, taught him the incantations and offerings that would appease the deities and ensure the beneficial rise of the Nile. They revealed to him the secrets of the stars, teaching him to read the celestial messages to foretell the events to come.

He was also prepared for the responsibilities of a pharaoh in terms of justice. Seated next to his father, Akhenaten observed the hearings where the plaintiffs came to present their disputes. He learned the delicate balance between law and compassion, between punishment and clemency. He was trained to be the ultimate judge, the one whose word would be the balance on which the acts of men would be weighed.

The architects and engineers of the kingdom showed him the plans of the great projects he should commission: majestic temples dedicated to the gods, colossal statues in his likeness to immortalize his glory, and monumental tombs where he would rest in the afterlife. Akhenaten learned to envision his reign as a link in the long chain of Egyptian history, each stone laid a testament to his divine will.

The generals taught him the art of war, not only to defend the borders of Egypt, but also to extend his influence. He practiced in the martial arts, wielding sword and bow with skill that inspired respect and admiration. He learned to command armies, to inspire courage in the hearts of his soldiers, and to lead them to victory.

Akhenaten was also trained in the art of governance. He was taught about the management of the kingdom's resources, about the importance of equitable wealth distribution to maintain society in harmony. He learned about each city, each temple, each agricultural domain, understanding that the prosperity of Egypt rested on the wisdom of his decisions.

Thus, day after day, Akhenaten drew closer to the crown of Egypt, growing in wisdom and stature, until the time came when he would be ready to assume the mantle of Pharaoh, to lead his people with justice and to inscribe his name among the greats of the eternal history of Egypt.

In the shadow of the palace's colonnades, young Akhenaten, heir to the throne of Egypt, immersed himself in the arcane of politics and the mysteries of spirituality. His days were rhythm by the lessons of the wise and the advice of the counselors, all determined to forge in him an exceptional pharaoh, a leader with a transcendent vision.

In parallel, the priests of Amun, holders of the keys to religious knowledge, initiated him into the secular rites that bound the pharaohs to the gods. But in the secret of his heart, Akhenaten felt a different call, a deep connection with Aten, the sun disk. He spent long hours in contemplation before the rays of the sun, feeling in him an unshakeable conviction that his destiny would be to revolutionize the faith of his ancestors.

Under the tutelage of the scholars, he studied ancient texts, seeking in the hieroglyphs carved on the walls of temples confirmation of his nascent beliefs. He savored the hymns that celebrated creation, and in the silence of the library, he composed his own verses, praises to Aten that foreshadowed the religious poetry he would one day introduce.

The political and spiritual formation of Akhenaten was not only a preparation for power, it was a personal quest, an inner journey towards a deeper understanding of the universe and his place in it as Pharaoh. He was preparing to become the bridge between heaven and earth, between the gods and men, and to guide his people towards a new era, under the benevolent gaze of Aten, whose golden rays promised illumination and truth.

In Thebes, the city of a hundred gates, the games of power and alliances wove a complex web, as dazzling and elusive as the reflections of the Nile at dusk. Akhenaten, young and still called Amenhotep IV, observed with increasing acuity the intricacies of the court, where every smile concealed an ambition and every gesture could be a symbol of challenge or submission.

The palace, with its vast halls with lotus-shaped columns and its courtyards open to the blue sky of Egypt, was the theater of an incessant ballet of courtiers, priests and dignitaries. Each one played his part in this symphony of power, seeking to influence Pharaoh Amenhotep III, the father of Akhenaten, and through him, the destinies of the empire.

Akhenaten, guided by his mentors, learned to decipher this subtle language. He understood that alliances were forged not only in the gilded salons, but also in the secret gardens of the harem, where the murmurings of women could redraw the maps of politics. He saw how the priests of Amun, with their oracles and their prophecies, could both support the throne and threaten it, if their interests were not preserved.

In the shadow of the colossal statues of past pharaohs, he met in secret those who shared his vision of a single cult centered on Aten. These alliances, forged in the common conviction and passion for a revolutionary religious ideal, would become the cornerstone of his future reign.

Akhenaten was not only a spectator of these power games; he was already a key player, weaving his own sons into the labyrinth of Thebes, preparing the ground for the advent of a new era. An era where the sun, with its pure and universal light, would sweep away the shadows of the old gods and establish a new order, with himself, Akhenaten, as the sole intermediary between Aten and his people.

In the silent depths of the Egyptian night, under the sparkling veil of a starry sky, Akhenaten, the future pharaoh, contemplated the immensity of the universe and nurtured in his heart dreams of a renewed empire. Far from indiscreet looks, in the solitude of his royal apartments, he let his mind wander to a future where Egypt would be transformed, not only in its political and social structure, but also in its very soul.

He imagined an empire where temples would no longer be dark labyrinths dedicated to a multitude of deities, but open spaces bathed in light, celebrating the glory of Aten, the sun disk. In his visions, the cities of Egypt flourished around vast courtyards and colonnades, where the people could gather to worship their one god under the blue sky, symbol of the infinite.

Akhenaten dreamed of art and architecture reflecting this new spirituality. He saw frescoes and bas-reliefs depicting life, fertility, and abundance offered by Aten. He envisioned statues representing him and his beautiful wife Nefertiti, not as distant and inaccessible beings, but as the divine couple embodying the benevolent proximity of the sun god.

In the field of diplomacy, he aspired to an empire that would be a beacon of wisdom and peace, radiating its power not through conquest, but through cultural influence and spiritual supremacy. He dreamed of caravans crossing endless deserts, bringing the world's treasures to the city of Akhetaten, the city of the horizon of Aten, which he planned to build.

These dreams of a renewed empire were for Akhenaten much more than simple aspirations, they were a promise to himself and to his people. A promise to break the chains of the old order and to inaugurate an era of light and truth, where every man, woman and child could live under the benevolent gaze of Aten, in an empire unified not only by land and blood, but by spirit and faith.

His avant-garde conceptions extended well beyond the boundaries of Thebes, the traditional capital. He envisioned a new city, Akhetaten "horizon of Aten", which would arise from the sand like a hymn to Aten. This city would be the embodiment of his revolutionary ideals, a place where architecture itself would sing the glory of the sun disk, with temples open to divine light and palaces whose clean lines would defy the canon of Egyptian art.

In the political arena, Akhenaten was preparing reforms that would upend the established order. He dreamed of dismantling the power of the priests of Amun, who held the reins of wealth and influence, to establish a monotheistic cult centered on Aten. His project was radical: a religion that would unify the people under one deity, eliminating the fragmentation and polytheism that had long dominated Egyptian spirituality.

He was also thinking about social reforms, envisioning a society where prosperity would be shared more equitably, where the arts would flourish freely, and where culture would be accessible to all, nobles and peasants. In his mind, art would no longer only serve to glorify gods and kings, but to celebrate everyday life and the intimate relationship between the people and the divine.

These reform projects, Akhenaten carried them within him as a sacred burden, a divine mission that consumed him day and night. He was ready to challenge the millennia-old traditions, to face the inevitable opposition, because he fervently believed in the light of Aten, in its ability to purify and renew the very heart of Egypt. In the silence of dawn, as the sun disk embraced the world with its first rays, Akhenaten sealed his commitment to these avant-garde conceptions that would soon shake the foundations of the old world.

The dawn was rising over Egypt, draping the Nile in a golden light, while Akhenaten, the future pharaoh, stood alone, absorbed in the vision of a reign that would forever mark the course of history. Akhenaten "he who is pleasing to Aten", whose very name was a tribute to the solar disk, Aten, dreamed of an empire illuminated by the wisdom and justice of this one god.

His ambition was great, as vast as the sky that the sun traverses every day. He envisioned a reign where Aten would not only be the center of Egyptian religion, but also the ethical and moral guide of society. Akhenaten did not simply want to be a pharaoh among others; he aspired to be the pharaoh of a new era, the founder of a spiritual revolution that would transform the relationship between the gods and men.

In his mind, each ray of Aten was a golden thread weaving a direct link between the sky and the earth, between the divine and the mortal. He saw his people bathed in this pure light, freed from the shadows of ignorance and superstition. Under his reign, Akhenaten promised a society where the truth of Aten would illuminate every aspect of life, where corruption and injustice would be swept away by the relentless light of day.

He imagined temples without ceilings, where the sunlight would enter without obstruction, altars without idols, where the offerings would be made directly to the splendor of Aten. Each day would be a celebration of life and light, each prayer a hymn to the glory of this creative force that nourishes and supports the universe.

However, Akhenaten's ambition was not without obstacles. He knew that his dream would meet resistance from traditional priests, nobles, and even the people, who were attached to the old gods and suspicious of this upheaval. Yet his conviction was unshakeable. With the quiet strength of someone who has been touched by a revelation, Akhenaten was ready to face these challenges, armed with his indomitable faith in Aten, ready to write his name in eternity as the pharaoh of a divine revolution.

The Advent of a New Era

In the golden sands of ancient Egypt, under the azure sky that embraces the horizon, a wind of change blows over the Nile. Akhenaten, whose very name evokes the sun disk, rises to power, bearing a vision that will defy the centuries. His ascent to the throne is a new dawn, an awakening of consciousness that resonates with the clarity of the dawn.

On the day of his coronation, the sky seems to open to celebrate the sacred union between the Pharaoh and the solar deity, Aten. The rays of the sun caress the majestic columns of the temples, as if to bless the beginning of his reign. The ceremonies are imbued with an unprecedented splendor, the chants and dances rise, mixing joy with reverence, while the incense sets the air ablaze with its heady scents.

Akhenaten stands before his people, his tall figure draped in luxurious linen, the double crown on his head, symbol of his authority over the Two Lands. His gaze, filled with an inner light, rests on the crowd gathered there. He speaks of a future where the many gods will give way to a single one, Aten, whose universal benevolence will flood every corner of the empire.

The proclamation of the religious revolution is a shock, a wave that spreads through cities and villages. Priests murmur, courtiers whisper, but the people listen, intrigued by this pharaoh who promises a personal and direct relationship with the divine. Akhenaten, with the quiet strength of one who has been touched by grace, embarks on the path of eternity, marking the beginning of an era that will be engraved in stone and in memories, as indelible as the hieroglyphs on the walls of the temples.

Egypt stands at a crossroads, between the respect of millennia-old traditions and the embrace of a reform that will upend the established order. It is the dawn of a new era, the advent of a heretical pharaoh, a visionary who challenges the gods to exalt only one, under the eternal gaze of Aten.

The enthronement of Akhenaten marks a decisive turning point in the millennia-long history of Egypt. The ceremony, bathed in the golden light of the rising sun, is a spectacle of divine grandeur. The priests, dressed in their long white robes, stand in a solemn procession, their chants rising to the sky as if to touch the gods themselves. But at the heart of this tradition, a stirring of rebellion sneaks in.

Akhenaten mounts the golden throne, his serene face turned towards the solar disk, Aten, of which he proclaims himself the unique son and prophet. He reveals his vision of a monotheistic cult, a bold break with the Egyptian polytheistic pantheon. The images of Amun and the other gods are removed, their names hammered out of the stone, an unthinkable act that shakes the very foundations of Egyptian theology.

The temples are emptied of their idols, the altars are stripped of their decorations, and the priests of Amun, once all-powerful, see their influence erode like sand under the desert wind. In their place, open temples, bathed in light, are erected in honor of Aten. The frescoes depict the pharaoh and his family under the benevolent rays of the sun, their hands outstretched in a gesture of love and reception.

This religious revolution is more than a transformation of beliefs; it is a declaration of spiritual independence, an act of faith that places Akhenaten and his people directly under the protection and providence of Aten. The faithful are encouraged to worship the sun not as a distant deity, but as a daily presence, a source of life and warmth that touches each individual without intermediaries.

In the streets of Thebes, the murmurs mix with astonishment. Some welcome the change with hope, others with deep fear. But all feel that Egypt is on the verge of entering a new era, under the leadership of a Pharaoh whose bold ideas will redefine what it means to be in communion with the divine. Akhenaten, with his great royal wife Nefertiti by his side as well as Akhenaten's brother, Thutmose grand vizier and Minister of Cults, stands ready to guide his people to an unknown future, under the benevolent and omnipresent gaze of Aten.

Akhenaten, proclaiming himself the son and the sole intercessor of Aten, establishes a radical monotheism. The traditional temples, with their dark sanctuaries and their mysterious statues, are abandoned in favor of vast open spaces where the sun can penetrate and illuminate the faithful. The hymns to Aten, poetic and fervent, celebrate life and creation, a hymn to nature and to its shining beauty.

The implications of this change are deep and multiple. On the religious level, the clergy of Amun, who had accumulated wealth and power, is shaken by the loss of its influence. The priests, formerly indispensable intermediaries between the gods and men, see their role called into question, their future uncertain.

On the social level, the cult of Aten promotes a form of connection more personal and direct with the divine. Akhenaten himself is often represented in a posture of intimacy and tenderness with his family, reflecting a more human and accessible image of royalty.

Politically, Akhenaten's religious reform is also a maneuver to centralize power in his hands. By eliminating the power of the priests of Amun and by erecting himself as the sole representative of Aten on earth, Akhenaten ensures an uncontested control over the religious and political aspects of Egypt.

However, this spiritual revolution is not without resistance. In the shadows of the colonnades of ancient temples, among the murmurs of the markets and the echoes of the working quarters, a tension is growing. Some followers remain attached to the old gods, secretly perpetuating the forbidden rites, while others fervently embrace the new doctrine.

Amarna (Akhetaten), the ephemeral city of the Aten horizon, rises from the sands in the fifth year of his reign as the materialized dream of Akhenaten, a visionary pharaoh who dared to defy the millennia-old traditions of Egypt. On the banks of the Nile, far from the ancient Thebes and its all-powerful priests, Akhenaten builds his new capital. Akhenaten had a set of sixteen monumental stelae erected surrounding the new city and defining its border.

The city, designed with a straight layout, a novelty for the time, stretches between the arid hills and the nourishing river. The palaces, open temples, and houses line up along vast avenues, bathed in light. The talatates (sandstone construction stone) were used for the quick construction of the new capital.

Amarna is a perpetual construction site, a metamorphosis of stone and stucco where each building reflects the divine will of Akhenaten. The frescoes and bas-reliefs depict the pharaoh and his family in scenes of daily life, a break with the idealized and frozen representation of previous rulers. Here, grace and naturalness replace the rigidity of conventions, and faces express emotion and individuality unknown until then.

The life in Amarna follows the rhythm of the sun. The artisans, the scribes, the servants and the nobles, all participate in the construction of this earthly utopia. The lush gardens, irrigated by ingenious canals, offer a green respite in the middle of the desert, symbolizing the life that Aten dispenses without distinction.

But Amarna is also the scene of political isolation. Halfway between Memphis, at the entrance of the Nile Delta, and Thebes, Amarna moves away from traditional centers of power, Akhenaten exposes himself to criticism and plots. Diplomatic correspondence, found in the form of clay tablets, testify to the tensions and challenges the Pharaoh must face, as the Egyptian empire is at a crossroads.

The city of Aten's Horizon is a bold dream, a vision that is almost modern in its approach to religion and society. But it is also a fragile dream, one that depends entirely on the will of one man to change the course of history. Amarna, with its temples open to the sky and its statues facing the sun, will remain in memory as the purest expression of Akhenaten's quest for a direct and intimate relationship with the divine, a place where each sunrise is a prayer and each sunset a poem in praise of Aten.

The construction of Amarna, the city dedicated to the worship of Aten, was an unprecedented feat, a race against time to create a metropolis ex nihilo in the Egyptian desert. Akhenaten, the heretical pharaoh, had chosen this virgin site to escape the influence of the priests of Amun and establish a religious and political center that would be entirely his own.

The workers, artisans, and architects came from all over Egypt, attracted by the promise of a grandiose project. The construction sites buzzed with activity from dawn, where sand and stone were transformed into temples, palaces, and houses.

The buildings rose quickly, thanks to innovative techniques and the rigorous organization of the work. The stones were transported by the Nile, cut, and assembled on site, while the stucco and paintings brought their touch of color and life to the buildings.

The daily life in Amarna was marked by the sun and the work. The inhabitants got up with the dawn to enjoy the morning freshness. The streets came to life, the markets opened their stalls, offering products from all over the empire: cereals, vegetables, fruits, Nile fish, meats and poultry, but also pottery, fabrics and jewelry.

The houses of Amarna, often simple and functional, were built around a central courtyard, offering a space of light and air. Families led a modest but comfortable existence there, the richest adorning their homes with colorful frescoes and indoor gardens.

The temples of Aten, without roofs, let divine light flood the sanctuaries. Religious ceremonies were moments of collective communion, where the people, gathered outdoors, could worship the sun directly, without intermediaries. Akhenaten himself, often accompanied by Queen Nefertiti and their daughters, took part in these rites, reinforcing his image as a Pharaoh accessible and close to his people.

But the city was not only a place of work and prayer. Art and culture also flourished there, freed from the rigid canons of the past. The artists of Amarna created revolutionary works, representing the royal family with astonishing expressiveness, capturing moments of tenderness and humanity.

However, life in Amarna was not without difficulties. The letters found, known as the Amarna archives, reveal complaints about delays in the delivery of grain or materials, conflicts between workers and administrators, and the logistical challenges of a city in constant expansion.

Amarna was a unique social and religious experience, a place where every day was a celebration of life under the benevolent gaze of Aten. But this city, built on the dreams and ideals of one man, was also vulnerable to the whims of politics and history.

The Amarna art, born under the impetus of Akhenaten, was an aesthetic revolution without precedent in the millennial history of Egypt. Breaking with the rigid conventions of traditional Egyptian art, it introduced a more natural, more fluid style that sought to capture the essence of life and the grace of the natural world.

In the Amarna workshops, the air was thick with the fine dust of limestone and echoed with the sound of chisels and hammers. The artists, inspired by the radical teachings of their pharaoh, were busy creating unprecedented representations of royalty and divinities. The statues and reliefs depicted Akhenaten, Nefertiti and their family with exaggerated and elongated features, full lips, prominent chins and bodies with slender, almost androgynous curves. These images were a celebration of individual beauty and uniqueness, a bold break with the impersonal idealization of royal figures from the past.

The murals, on the other hand, were full of bright colors and scenes of daily life, illustrating with detailed precision the luxurious gardens, animals, banquets and religious rituals. The artists of Amarna dared to represent intimate moments of the royal family, such as Akhenaten and Nefertiti playing with their daughters, a striking contrast with the formal and distant representations of the sovereigns in previous eras.

The Amarna art was also revolutionary in its representation of the sun, Aten. Unlike the traditionally human or hybrid represented Egyptian deities, Aten was illustrated simply by a solar disk whose rays ended in benevolent hands "Ankh", offering life and prosperity. This symbolic simplicity marked a deep break with the complex pantheon of ancient Egypt and highlighted the direct relationship between the god and his followers.

However, this period of artistic innovation was also a reflection of the tensions and contradictions of the time. Behind the beauty of the works, one could sometimes perceive a certain anxiety, a feeling of urgency and fragility. The artists, although free to explore new forms and ideas, worked under the demanding gaze of a pharaoh who was both their patron and the main subject of their art.

The Religious Revolution of Akhenaten was a spiritual cataclysm that shook the millennia-old foundations of Egypt. At the heart of this storm of change stood Akhenaten, the visionary pharaoh, the architect of a new era who sought to remodel the religious consciousness of his people.

Thutmose, Akhenaten's brother, was an enigmatic figure, often overshadowed by the immense figure of the heretical pharaoh. Yet, behind the scenes of power, he played a crucial role, acting as vizier and minister of cults, and thus becoming a key pillar of Akhenaten's religious revolution.

The link between the two brothers was woven of complexity and intimacy. Thutmose, with his sharp mind and impeccable education, had been the childhood companion of Akhenaten, sharing with him the lessons of the wise and the games in the luxurious gardens of the palace. As destiny led them on different paths, one towards the throne and the other towards the administration of the kingdom, their shared vision for Egypt remained unshakeable.

As vizier, Thutmose was the hand that executed the pharaoh's will. He oversaw major construction projects, managed state affairs, and above all, orchestrated the delicate transition from ancient cults to Aten's monotheism. It was a role that required iron diplomacy and unshakeable faith in his brother's ideals, as he often had to face opposition from traditional priests and nobility.

The Minister of Cults, a position of prestige and power, had become under Thutmose an instrument of change. He had the herculean task of redefining Egyptian spirituality, transforming rituals and reeducating the people. He had to make sure that the worship of Aten was not only accepted, but embraced with fervor by the masses.

Thutmose was also Akhenaten's accomplice in the creation of Amarna, the radiant city dedicated to Aten. He made sure that every stone, every column, every statue breathed the philosophy of the solar cult. Under his supervision, Amarna became a living symbol of the religious revolution, a testament of stone and light to the ambition of the two brothers.

Thutmose, the brother, the vizier, and the accomplice, remains an elusive figure, but his shadow looms over the ruins of Amarna, reminding those who pass through its silent gates that behind every great leader is often an equally great advisor, whose actions shape history in the shadow of the throne.

Nefertiti: The Great Royal Wife

The queen of Egypt, often seen as a figure in the shadows, was actually a powerful force in the kingdom, especially during the time of Akhenaten. Her influence extended far beyond the secret chambers and corridors of the palace. She was the companion of the pharaoh, his equal, and the mother of his daughters Meritaten, Meketaten, Ankhesenpaaten, Neferneferuaten Tasherit, Neferneferure, Setepenre.

In the context of Akhenaten's religious revolution, Queen Nefertiti, daughter of Ay, and later her daughters and other royal wives, played crucial roles. Nefertiti in particular was often represented at the same scale as the Pharaoh, a sign of her exceptional status. She was not only the Great Royal Wife, but also a priestess of Aten, and her face was as revered as her husband's.

The representations of the queen in Amarna art were revolutionary. She was depicted with a grace and presence that defied the artistic conventions of the time. Her features, like those of Akhenaten, were stylized with elongated curves and an elegance that reflected the new religious aesthetic. She was often shown participating actively in religious rites, sometimes even leading ceremonies or offering sacrifices.

The Aten cult itself gave an important place to the royal family. The queen, as well as the princesses, were integrated into solar theology. They were the earthly representatives of the deity, intermediaries between the sun god and the people. This representation was a radical change from previous traditions, where queens were important but rarely placed on an equal footing with the pharaoh in public worship.

The queen was also a symbol of fertility and dynastic continuity. In an empire where the royal lineage was the cornerstone of political stability, she was the guardian of the future. Her children were the heirs to the throne of Egypt and the future representatives of the god Aten on earth.

In addition, the queen played a diplomatic role. Marriages were often used as political tools, and the queen could be a foreign princess whose alliance strengthened ties between Egypt and other powers. Her correspondence with other royal courts was an essential part of international diplomacy.

In the temples of Aten, images of the queen, with her long flowing robes and high crown, were ubiquitous. She was both a vision of ideal beauty and a pillar of the new religious order. Her representation in art and her role in worship were clear messages: the queen was not just the mother or wife of the pharaoh, she was an integral part of the solar deity, a living aspect of Aten himself.

Thus, in the midst of the Akhenaten revolution, the queen was both an icon and an influence, a priestess and a politician, a mother and a monarch. Her representation in art and her role in the cult reflected the complexity and power of her position, making her a central figure in one of the most fascinating periods of Egyptian history.

The disappearance of Queen Nefertiti remains one of the greatest mysteries of ancient Egyptian history. Her presence, so dominant in the early years of Akhenaten's reign, seems to vanish suddenly from the historical record, leaving Egyptologists and historians in a state of perpetual speculation.

Imagine the corridors of the Amarna palace, where the whispers of the servants and the courtiers mix with the echoes of the chants dedicated to Aten. Queen Nefertiti, once the center of this religious and political excitement, is no longer visible. Her apartments, once filled with the aroma of the finest incense and the sounds of delicate music, are now silent, as if a shadow had enveloped her existence.

Theories abound about what could have happened to the queen. Some suggest she fell from grace, perhaps because of an internal power struggle or a change in religious affairs. Others argue that she may have died, perhaps suddenly, leaving behind a power vacuum and a broken hearted people.

The frescoes and reliefs that once depicted her alongside her husband in scenes of devotion and familial happiness no longer give new representations. The artisans who sculpted her face with such adoration seem to have put their scissors to rest. The priests who sang her praises alongside Akhenaten no longer pronounce her name in their prayers.

There are rumors in the markets and temples: some say she was exiled, there are those who whisper that she was taken by a disease, leaving behind her daughters and a grieving Pharaoh, isolated in his religious convictions.

Archaeological excavations have tried to penetrate the veil of this mystery, seeking in tombs and ruins clues that could reveal the destiny of the queen. But so far, no conclusive discovery has been made, and the true story of the end of Nefertiti remains hidden, buried perhaps forever under the sands of the desert or the strata of history.

In the dreams of poets and the stories of storytellers, Nefertiti always lives, a legendary queen whose beauty and power continue to fascinate. But in the annals of history, her absence remains an enigmatic silence, a void that defies explanation, a mystery that continues to defy time.

Merytaton: The Heiress Princess

Meritaten, raised in the revolutionary atmosphere of Amarna, was not only the eldest daughter of Akhenaten and Nefertiti, but also the one who took over as Great Royal Wife after her mother's disappearance. Her role as Great Royal Wife was crucial in the continuity of her father's reign and in the perpetuation of the new religion focused on the worship of Aten.

In the corridors of the palace, where the murals depicted the royal family bathed in the divine light of Aten, Meritaten stood alongside Akhenaten, sharing the responsibilities of the crown. She was often represented in the art of the time, her slender silhouette and fine features evoking the beauty and power of her mother, Nefertiti.

Her presence at official ceremonies and in religious rituals was a symbol of dynastic continuity and the legitimacy of the worship of Aten. Meritaten, as Great Royal Wife, played a diplomatic and religious role, reinforcing alliances through strategic marriages and serving as an intermediary between the Pharaoh and his people.

Meritaten embodied the essence of Amarna royalty, a fusion of political power and religious devotion, her very existence an ode to the revolution her father had initiated.

In the archives of history, the role of Meritaten as Great Royal Wife remains shrouded in mystery, as does the end of her story. But in the moments when she held her role, she was the guardian of the flame of Aten, the protector of her parents' legacy, and perhaps the bearer of hope for the future of a dynasty faced with the inevitable change of the winds of history.

The question of succession to the Egyptian throne was of paramount importance, and in the tumultuous context of the end of Akhenaten's reign, it took on an even more critical dimension. Meritaten, as Great Royal Wife and eldest daughter of the Pharaoh, was at the heart of these dynastic concerns. She embodied the continuity of the royal bloodline and was seen as a potential pivot for the future stability of Egypt.

In the halls of the Amarna palace, the counselors murmured about the future of the royal line, while the priests of Aten prayed for divine clarity. Meritaten, with her youth and position, was often at the center of these discussions, her marriage and progeny being subjects of speculation and political maneuvering.

Marriage alliances were an essential tool for reinforcing ties with foreign powers and Egyptian nobles. Meritaten, by virtue of her position, could play a key role in these unions, thus ensuring the dissemination and longevity of Akhenaten's influence and religious reform.

The question of her descent was also crucial. The birth of a male heir would be a sign of stability and continuity, while a line of princesses would raise the question of succession and legitimacy. The texts and representations of the time hint at the pressure that weighed on the shoulders of Meritaten, the need to give birth to an heir who could wear the double crown of Egypt.

In the gardens of Amarna, where flowers bloomed under the sun of Aten, Meritaten often had to meditate on her role in the future of the empire. She was both a symbol of the old order and the promise of an uncertain future. Her life, woven into the complex fabric of politics, religion and tradition, was a reflection of Egypt itself, at the crossroads between a glorious past and an unknown future.

The end of Akhenaten's reign was approaching, and with it, the end of an era. Meritaten stood on the threshold of history, her destiny inextricably linked to that of her country. Her role as Great Royal Wife and potential mother of the next Pharaoh was a last bastion against the shifting sands of time, an attempt to maintain order in a world in transformation.

The Twilight of Akhenaten's Reign

The reign of Akhenaten, marked by radical changes and bold reforms, was not without challenges, both within the borders of Egypt and beyond. These challenges shaped his time and left an indelible mark on the history of the ancient empire.

Inside the kingdom, the religious revolution initiated by Akhenaten upended the established order. The closure of temples dedicated to the old gods and the exclusive promotion of the worship of Aten caused a shockwave among the priests and the faithful of traditional cults. The priests of Amun, in particular, who enjoyed considerable power and wealth, found themselves dispossessed and marginalized, creating a potential hotbed of discontent and resistance.

The changes in art and culture, although innovative, greatly disturbed those who were attached to classical conventions. The more naturalistic and sometimes strange representations, the themes focused on the royal family and sunlight, all of this constituted a break with the centuries-old aesthetic norms.

On the administrative level, the relocation of the capital to Amarna required complex logistics and a considerable investment. Resources were diverted to build the new city, and the bureaucracy had to adapt to a rapidly changing environment.

Beyond the borders, Akhenaten's Egypt was facing increasing tensions. The diplomatic correspondence, known as the Amarna archives, reveal a period of turbulence in international relations. The vassal kingdoms in Syria and

Canaan, traditionally under Egyptian influence, complained of neglect and the lack of military support in the face of enemy aggression, including the Hittites.

The great powers of the time, such as the Mitanni and the Hatti, observed with interest and sometimes with concern the changes in Egypt, wondering how these upheavals would affect the regional balance of power.

In this context, Akhenaten seemed focused on his religious and cultural projects, perhaps to the detriment of foreign affairs and the defense of distant territories. The increasingly desperate missives of vassal kings testify to a period of uncertainty and unresolved conflicts.

The reign of Akhenaten, with its high ideals and utopian aspirations, thus collided with the reality of a complex and merciless world. The internal challenges, related to religious and cultural reform, as well as the external threats, coming from an empire that was extending over increasingly contested territories, wove the backdrop of a reign that would remain in memory as one of the most controversial and fascinating in Egyptian history.

In the declining years of Akhenaten's reign, the waters of the great Nile River, source of all life in Egypt, became capricious. The annual floods, once so regular and generous, became erratic, insufficient, plunging the kingdom into a period of famine and despair. The grain silos, usually swollen with abundant harvests, emptied, while the thirsty fields yielded only meager and unsatisfactory crops.

The people, whose survival depended on the benefits of the Nile, began to murmur against the pharaoh and his one god, Aten. In the streets of the cities and the alleys of the markets, it was whispered that the traditional gods, neglected and forgotten, were taking revenge. The priests of the ancient cults, relegated to the margins of society by the religious revolution of Akhenaten, found in these calamities a proof of their warning: Egypt could not prosper without the support of the whole of its divine pantheon.

The wars at the borders, the plague, and now the famine, everything seemed to converge towards a crisis of faith. The faithful of Aten, once fervent, started to doubt, while the supporters of the old gods became bolder, feeding the flame of the revolt against the solar cult. Akhenaten, once visionary, found himself isolated, his authority shaken not only by the political and military challenges, but also by the merciless forces of nature that seemed to conspire against his reign.

In the hearts of Egyptians, fear took root, and with it, the ardent desire for a return to the old order, to a time when multiple gods watched over the Nile and ensured the stability and prosperity of the land of the pharaohs. Akhenaten, faced with this deep crisis, was on the edge of a precipice, his dream of an empire under the sign of Aten threatened by the growing whispers of a starving and desperate people.

The progressive restoration of ancient cults in Egypt after the reign of Akhenaten is a fascinating transitional period, marked by a return to traditions and a reaffirmation of the gods who had been neglected during the Amarna period. This movement was not only a political or religious reaction, but also an attempt to restore the cosmic order, which many believed had been disrupted by Akhenaten's radical reforms.

In the corridors of power, at the end of the reign of Akhenaten and more explicitly under the reign of his son, the young Tutankhamun, efforts to reintegrate the ancient deities began to take shape. The abandoned temples were reopened and the cults reactivated. The priests of Amun, whose power had been shaken under Akhenaten, quickly regained their influence and their privileges.

On the symbolic level, the restoration of the ancient cults was manifested by the renovation and reopening of the temples, the resumption of religious processions and festivals, and the reinscription of the names of the gods that had been erased from public monuments. The images of Aten were replaced or modified to once again represent the plurality of Egyptian deities.

Economically, the restoration of traditional cults also meant the rehabilitation of the economic networks associated with the temples. The temples were not only places of worship, but also centers of production, storage and redistribution of wealth. Their agricultural lands, workshops and stores played a crucial role in the Egyptian economy.

Politically, the restoration of the ancient cults strengthened the position of the pharaohs who followed Akhenaten. By presenting themselves as restorers of the traditional order, they legitimized their reign and strengthened their authority. Neferneferuaten Tasherit and Tutankhamun, in particular, although young and probably influenced by advisers, are often credited with initiating this movement back to the sources.

This period saw a return to classical artistic and literary forms, after the radical experimentation of the Amarna period. The representations of gods and pharaohs resumed the idealized standards and stylized proportions that had been characteristic of Egyptian art before Akhenaten.

The restoration of ancient cults was not immediate or uniform, and some aspects of the cult of Aten survived, discreetly integrating into the Egyptian pantheon. However, the general trend was clear: a return to the old order, perceived as a guarantee of stability and continuity in a world where religion was inseparable from the identity and social structure of ancient Egypt.

Neferneferuaten Tasherit: A Pharaoh in the Shadow

Neferneferouaton Tasherit, often overshadowed by the fame of her illustrious parents Akhenaten and Nefertiti, is a figure shrouded in mystery in the history of ancient Egypt. Her life, like a palimpsest fresco, reveals the complex layers of politics, religion, and female power during a period of unprecedented upheaval.

In the intimacy of the palaces of Amarna, Neferneferuaten Tasherit grows under the benevolent shadow of the sun disk, Aten, whose revolutionary cult permeates her education and her vision of the world. She is trained in the delicate arts of the court, but also in the subtleties of solar theology, which places her father as the exclusive prophet of a single god.

On the political front, her youth is marked by the intrigues and maneuvering that stir the court. Her name, which means "The beauties of Aten are perfect," is a living tribute to the new religion. She witnesses the tension between the supporters of the old order and the fervent followers of the Aten cult, a struggle that shapes her destiny.

Her ascent to power is as sudden as it is unexpected. Upon her father's death, the question of succession arises sharply. Neferneferuaten Tasherit is propelled onto the political stage, perhaps first as a regent or co-regent, before potentially taking the title of Pharaoh in her own right.

In the role of sovereign, she must navigate the troubled waters of an empire in search of identity. Her reign, although short, is a pivotal period where the decisions made will have lasting repercussions on the future of Egypt. She is forced to juggle between the preservation of the Amarna heritage and the increasing pressures for a return to traditions.

Her legacy is complex, marked by the controversies and hypotheses of Egyptologists. She probably is the enigmatic Smenkhkare, a Pharaoh whose nature and gender remain debated. Others argue that she could have ruled alone, before ceding the throne to Tutankhamun, the young Pharaoh who would make an impression with his death more than his political accomplishments.

The end of her reign and the circumstances of her death are shrouded in mystery. Her name is erased, her monuments usurped or destroyed, as if to erase her passage from history. Yet the figure of Neferneferuaten Tasherit remains engraved in the collective memory, not as a mere echo of her parents, but as the symbol of a transitional period, where a woman was able, even briefly, to hold the reins of power in one of the greatest civilizations of antiquity.

The reign of Neferneferuaten Tasherit, although brief, stands as a fragile bridge between the radical era of Akhenaten and the return to tradition under Tutankhamun. She inherits a kingdom in full effervescence, an empire shaken by religious reforms and drastic political changes.

In the corridors of power, she is confronted with the immense task of consolidating her father's legacy while appeasing the tensions that threaten to tear the very fabric of Egyptian society. The priests of Amun, dispossessed and furious, murmur in the shadows, aspiring to restore their former glory. The nobles, whose influence has been eroded by the exclusive worship of Aten, seek to regain their lost power.

On the international stage, Akhenaten's Egypt, once a feared power, has seen its influence wane. Vassal kingdoms are becoming increasingly bold in their claims of independence. Neferneferuaten Tasherit must navigate these turbulent waters, trying to preserve alliances and maintain the empire.

Her political impact is intrinsically linked to these challenges. She may have tried to reform the cult of Aten, to make it less exclusive, in the hope of reconciling the conflicting factions. Some evidence suggests that she might have initiated a cautious return to polytheism, an attempt at compromise to reunify a fractured country.

The scope of her reign is often evaluated through the prism of the actions of his successors. Tutankhamun, in particular, is known for having overturned the Amarna reforms and restored traditional cults. This could indicate that Neferneferuaten Tasherit's efforts to balance old traditions and the new cult were only partially successful, or perhaps too late to take root.

In the end, the short reign of Neferneferuaten Tasherit is testimony to the complexity of governing a society in full mutation. Her political impact, although perhaps eclipsed by the more visible actions of her predecessors and successors, lies in her attempt to navigate a period of transition, to maintain the unity of an empire under tension, and to lay the foundations on which her successors could build. Her reign is a footnote in the annals of history, but a footnote that resonates with the echoes of a pivotal moment, a moment when ancient Egypt stood at the crossroads between past and future.

The figure of Neferneferuaten Tasherit, often enveloped in the veil of mystery, stands at the crossroads of the tumultuous paths of Egyptian history. Her reign, ephemeral and enigmatic, is dotted with unanswered questions, historical silences that raise as much curiosity as conjecture.

The governance of Neferneferuaten Tasherit is an incomplete puzzle, with missing pieces that could reveal the true nature of her administration. The texts and reliefs that have survived offer fragmentary glimpses, suggesting that she may have tried to maintain the precarious balance established by her predecessor, Akhenaten. However, the details of her policies, her reforms, or even her struggles to establish her authority remain fuzzy, lost in the sands of time.

The mysteries of her death are just as troubling. No tomb clearly identified as hers has been discovered, no detailed account of her last days has survived. This historical silence fuels the theories: did she die of a sudden illness, was she a victim of a court conspiracy, or was she eclipsed by the return of the priests of Amun? The truth remains elusive, hidden somewhere in the shadows of history. Could her tomb be behind the funeral chamber of Tutankhamun?

The consequences of her reign are just as difficult to discern. If she reigned as a co-regnant or sole sovereign, did she manage to leave a lasting impression on Egyptian politics, or was her passage too brief to counter the powerful currents that sought to erase the Amarna legacy?

The transition to Tutankhamun, her successor, suggests that the reign of Neferneferuaten Tasherit may have been a transitional period, a moment of respite before the old gods regained their preeminent place. Her death could have marked the definitive end of the Amarna experience, leaving behind an empire ready to reconnect with its glorious past.

In general, the governance and death of Neferneferuaten Tasherit remain among the great mysteries of ancient Egypt.

Every archaeological discovery related to this period is scrutinized in the hope of finding clues, every text is analyzed in search of subtexts that could shed light on its history. Until new evidence comes to light, the true story of Neferneferuaten Tasherit will remain an enigma, a fascinating but incomplete chapter of pharaonic history.

The transition to Tutankhamun, the young pharaoh who would restore the ancient gods to their former glory, marked the end of a bold experiment in religion and art. The temples of Aten were abandoned, the Amarna frescoes were covered, and the prayers to Amun echoed again under the vaults of the millennia-old sanctuaries.

Thus, the transition to a new chapter was complete, not with a great flourish, but with the soft rustle of a page turning, ready to be written by the hand of destiny.

In the silent corridors of the Amarna palace, where the echoes of Akhenaten's revolution still resonated, the question of succession was raised with a muted urgency. The management of this transition was a balancing act played on the tightrope of history, where each movement could either restore balance or plunge the kingdom into chaos.

The court was divided, alliances were made and broken like the sands of the desert, and every decision made by Neferneferuaten Tasherit was scrutinized for signs of weakness or strength. She had to honor her father's legacy while recognizing the winds of change blowing through the land.

In this charged atmosphere, succession was not only a matter of royal lineage, but also of political vision. The young pharaoh, with the wisdom that surpassed her age, sought to balance the traditions of the past with the necessities of the present. She knew that Egypt must turn towards a future where the many gods would be worshipped once again, where the temples would be restored to their former splendor, and where the people could find comfort in the familiar.

Despite this, the task was Herculean. Each day brought its share of challenges, each decision its weight of consequences. Neferneferuaten Tasherit, in her heart, hoped that the transition to Tutankhamun, the young pharaoh who waited in the shadows, would be gentle. She dreamed of a united, strong, and prosperous Egypt, but the gods, as always, had their own designs.

The delicate management of the succession was a silent ballet, a dance of shadow and light, played on the stage of the world for an audience of immortals. And as Neferneferuaten Tasherit placed the crown on the head of her successor, she knew that her role in history was both ephemeral and eternal, a golden thread woven into the great carpet of Egypt.

The closure of the Amarna chapter was a melancholy goodbye to a time of bold dreams and radical changes. The city of Amarna, once vibrant under the reign of Akhenaten, began to lose its essence, as if the sun of Aten itself was withdrawing, leaving behind lengthened shadows on the colonnades and frescoes that had celebrated the glory of a single god.

The followers of the Aten cult, those who had followed Akhenaten in his quest for a reformed spirituality, looked on with resigned sadness as their reality was gradually dismantled. The temples that had echoed with hymns to Aten were now silent, their altars abandoned, their priests dispersed. The religious revolution, which had shaken the very foundations of Egypt, now seemed to vanish like a mirage in the desert.

The return to Thebes was inevitable, a movement orchestrated by the priests of Amun and the royal counselors who saw in the restoration of the ancient gods a way to restore order and stability. The transition was orchestrated with precision that was meant to be reassuring to the people, an unspoken promise that the days of upheaval were over.

Thebes, with its majestic temples and colossal statues, was ready to resume its role as spiritual and political capital. The processions resumed, the incense burned again in the censers, and the chants in honor of Amun filled the air, as if the city itself were breathing fully again.

The closure of the Amarna chapter did not mean the forgetting of the years under the sun of Aten. The ideas of Akhenaten had sown seeds that would continue to germinate in the minds and hearts, even under the cover of orthodoxy. But for the moment, Egypt was looking to the past to find its future, and Thebes shone again as the beacon of civilization, guiding the people towards calmer waters.

In this transition, there was both an end and a new beginning, the end of an era marked by experimentation and the beginning of another, seeking to reconnect with tradition. And while the last vestiges of Amarna were carried away by the wind, Egypt turned to Thebes, to the gods who had shaped its history, ready to write the next chapter of its eternal saga.

Thutmose and the exodus

Thutmose, Akhenaten's brother and former vizier and minister of the cult, still believes in a monotheistic religion and one God. For him, the worship of the one unique god, the god of the solar disk, must continue. He therefore refuses to return to Thebes and honor the ancient gods.

The exodus of Thutmose with his disciples to the promised land was an episode shrouded in mystery and legend, a story that would span the ages and inspire generations. Thutmose, brother of Akhenaten and fervent defender of the Cult of Aten, refused to abandon the light of the one god, even in the face of the irresistible rise of the traditional Egyptian pantheon.

As the shadows lengthened over Amarna and the echoes of the hymns to Aten faded, Thutmose gathered around him those who, like him, could not deny their faith. They were men and women of conviction, artisans, scribes, priests and entire families, all united by the belief in a god who shone above all others.

Their departure was a journey through merciless deserts, under a blazing sun that seemed to guide them and test them at the same time. They left the city of Amarna, taking with them the teachings of Akhenaten, the prayers and the hopes of a life dedicated to Aten. Their trip was a quest for freedom, a flight from the persecution and the return of the old gods that threatened to erase their faith.

Thutmose, who became Moses in the desert wind, led his disciples with the determination of a prophet. He was both their guide and their guardian, the one who carried the light of Aten in his heart like an unquenchable torch. They crossed arid lands, steep mountains and lost valleys, always to the east, to the promised land where they could worship Aten without fear.

Their exodus was marked by trials, moments of doubt and despair, but also by moments of grace where the presence of Aten was manifested in the simplicity of an oasis or in the purity of a starry sky. Each step was an act of faith, each day an affirmation of their commitment to the god who had changed their lives.

The legend of their journey would cross time, intertwining with other beliefs and traditions, becoming an integral part of the fabric of religious history. The Exodus of Thutmose and his disciples would become a powerful symbol of resilience and man's eternal quest for spiritual freedom.

And as they moved away from Amarna, the city of the sun emptied of its essence behind them, but in front of them an horizon of possibilities opened up, a new chapter where Aten would be worshipped in the purity of his cult, far from the machinations and intrigues of the temples of Thebes.

At the beginning of the exodus, the people had to cross the vast desert expanses of Egypt. The desert was an inhospitable and merciless environment, filled with sand, heat, and dangers such as snakes and scorpions. The people had to face many challenges to cross these desert regions, but they were guided by Moses and his faith in God. He crossed the Reed Sea, also called the Red Sea, by a fierce east wind that dried up the body of water, and thus the waters were divided.

Later, the people reached the mountains of Sinai. The mountains were an even more hostile environment than the desert, but the people were able to cross them through the faith and determination of Moses.

Finally, the Hebrew people reached the Promised Land and discovered a green and fertile country, full of forests, hills, and rivers. It was an amazing and wonderful landscape that gave the people hope and the strength to continue building a new nation.

The Posterity of Amarna

The posterity of Amarna, enveloped in the diaphanous veils of history, is a persistent echo of the greatness and audacity of a dream that defied the heavens. The ruins of the city, bathed in the golden light of the setting sun, are the silent witnesses of a bygone era, when a Pharaoh dared to imagine a world under the aegis of a single god.

The ruins of Amarna tell the story of a revolution, not only religious but also artistic and social, which shook the foundations of ancient Egypt. The frescoes, sculptures and stelae, although mutilated by time and forgetfulness, still bear the traces of a new aesthetics, a vision that transcended conventions to seek truth in simplicity and emotion.

The descendants of Amarna, dispersed like seeds in the wind, carried with them the germs of these revolutionary ideas. In the following generations, artists, thinkers, and believers sometimes found, as if by a collective memory, the echo of this period when man had approached divinity not through a pantheon of mythical figures, but through the medium of a benevolent and universal sun.

The posterity of Amarna is also that of its illustrious inhabitants: Akhenaten, Nefertiti, their daughters, and the faithful who shared their vision. Their names, engraved in stone and recorded in the annals of history, have survived attempts at erasure and centuries of silence. They still resonate today as symbols of courage and innovation, reminding those who evoke them that history is often written by those who dare to challenge the status quo.

The ideas of Amarna, although suppressed and removed in the years following the fall of the city, survived in transformed forms, perhaps influencing, according to some scholars, the first monotheisms that emerged in the region. The quest for a single god, for a personal and direct relationship with the divine, finds a distant reflection in the teachings that flourished long after the disappearance of Amarna.

Thus, the posterity of Amarna is not only a question of material inheritance, but also of spiritual and intellectual inheritance. It is an invitation to contemplate the audacity of those who dreamed of a different world, and to recognize that, sometimes, the greatest changes take root in the most improbable visions.

Chapter IV. Tutankhamun: The Child Pharaoh and the Restoration

The Reintegration of Traditional Deities

The reintegration of traditional deities into the beating heart of Egypt was not simply a return to the old order, but a delicate dance between past and present, orchestrated with subtle grace by Neferneferuaten Tasherit. She, the daughter of light, had grown up in the lengthened shadow of Aten, but understood that the roots of her people plunged into a fertile land of myths and legends that could not be uprooted without the very soul of Egypt withering.

In the temples where silence had reigned during the reign of Akhenaten, the priests began to murmur the forgotten incantations again, waking the gods who were asleep in the corners of the collective memory. The statues of Isis, Osiris, Hathor and Amun, which had been neglected, were dusted off and restored, their stone faces welcoming the faithful again.

Neferneferuaten Tasherit, like a mediator between times, did not seek to erase the past but to weave it with the present, creating a set of beliefs that could envelop her people in a mantle of renewed spirituality. She did not deny Aten, but placed him among the other gods, as a brother rather than an absolute sovereign.

The processions resumed in the city streets, the sacred chants rose up to the heavens once again, and the offerings filled the air with their sweet scents. The gods, in their multitude, regained their place in the daily lives of the

Egyptians, and the wheel of religious life began to turn again, as inevitable and reassuring as the cycle of the Nile.

The reintegration of traditional deities was thus an act of reconciliation, a symphony where each note, old or new, found its place to create harmony that resonated with the soul of an eternal people. Neferneferuaten Tasherit, in her wisdom, knew that the identity of a nation does not reside in the effacement of the past, but in its ability to embrace its entire history, with its ruptures and its continuities, its shadows and its lights.

The end of the Amarna Period and its consequences

The end of the Amarna period was like the twilight of a long, tumultuous day, where the shadows of great ideas and revolutions stretched until they blended into the darkness of forgetfulness. The city of Amarna, once vibrant under the reign of Akhenaten, began to lose its essence, its inhabitants leaving the once lively streets to return to the old centers of power.

The temples of Aten, purified and bathed in light, emptied little by little, giving way to a heavy silence, as if the echoes of prayers and hymns had been carried away by the wind of the desert. The revolutionary frescoes, with their bold and intimate representations of the royal family, began to fade under the relentless assault of the sun.

With the disappearance of Neferneferuaten Tasherit and the return to Thebes, the cult of Aten was gradually abandoned, and the priests of Amun regained their preeminent place, restoring the rites and ceremonies that had been suppressed. The wealth and resources that had been dedicated to the new capital and its single god were reassigned to the traditional temples, in an effort to restore the old order and pacify the gods who had been neglected.

The return to Thebes marked a conscious effort to erase the traces of the Amarna heresy. The statues and monuments erected in honor of Akhenaten and his family were dismantled, their names hammered out of history, in an attempt to erase them from the collective memory. It was a damnatio memoriae, a condemnation of memory, which aimed to purge Egypt of the Amarna interlude as one erases a troubling dream upon waking.

However, the impact of this period could not be completely eradicated. The ideas of Akhenaten, although suppressed, continued to murmur in the corridors of time, secretly influencing future generations. The artists, having tasted the freedom of expression and the novelty of the Amarnian style, could not completely return to the rigid and idealized forms of the past. A subtle change had taken place, infusing a touch of realism and humanity into Egyptian art.

The end of the Amarna period was therefore a complex mixture of loss and recovery, destruction and rebirth. It left behind a legacy of questioning and spiritual research, a memory of what a Pharaoh's audacity had dared to challenge, and a reminder that even the gods could be questioned.

In the quicksand of time, under the azure sky of ancient Egypt, the story of a prince born of the shadow of a revolution is woven. In the heart of the Nile Valley, where the waters of life murmur the secrets of the gods, Beketaten, the enigmatic sister of the heretical pharaoh Akhenaten, bears within her the heir of a crumbling empire. This son, destined for greatness, is Tutankhamun, whose very name is a distant echo of forgotten deities.

The birth of this prince, shrouded in mystery like the dunes shroud buried treasure, is a balm for the hearts of the faithful, perhaps a sign that the gods have not abandoned

Egypt to its fate. In the royal apartments, where the scents of incense mix with the sweet smells of the lotus, Beketaten, the young lady, gazes at her son with a mixture of joy and apprehension. The walls, painted with scenes of hunting and fertility, are silent witnesses to the end of one era and the beginning of another.

Tutankhamun, whose eyes barely open on the world, is already carrying a heavy legacy. The priests, with whispers as light as the linen of their clothes, scrutinize the auguries and the divine signs, looking for the will of the gods in the entrails of the sacrifices. They hope that this prince, born of the lineage of Akhenaten but raised under the aegis of the ancient traditions, will be the one who reconciles the past with the future.

The first cries of the prince resound in the palace like the song of a new era, a sweet-bitter melody that carries with it the promise of a return to the old order and the fear of an uncertain future. The young mother, surrounded by her maids and advisers, knows that her son is destined to be more than a mere mortal; he is the bridge between two worlds, that of his father, marked by the single sun of Aten, and that of the many gods who have shaped Egypt since the dawn of time.

In the hanging gardens of the palace, where the song of the birds mixes with the rustling of the palms, Beketaten whispers prayers for her son. She implores Hathor, goddess of motherhood, to watch over this small being whose life is a golden thread woven into the great tapestry of Egyptian dynasties. She knows that, despite the turmoil that is shaking the kingdom, Tutankhamun is a ray of hope, a lighthouse in the night that guides Egypt towards a destiny still written in the stars.

This is the beginning of the story of Tutankhamun, forgotten prince, child of light and darkness, whose name will be carved in stone and the hearts of men for eternity.

Within the palaces of Thebes, where the columns rise like petrified prayers towards the infinite sky, the young Tutankhamun grows in the shadow of the mysteries of his birth. Son of Beketaten, the enigmatic sister of Akhenaten, his origin is wrapped in the mist of an untold story, a secret whispered by the hot winds of the desert and kept by the immutable sphinxes.

The first years of the prince are rocked by the stories of the priests and the melodies of the golden harps, while the dancers with diaphanous veils evoke, through their movements, the legends of the gods. Tutankhamun, whose eyes sparkle with insatiable curiosity, learns to walk on the precious carpets that cover the fresh floors of the royal apartments, under the benevolent gaze of the statues of illustrious ancestors.

The gardens of the palace, where lotuses bloom in an aquatic ballet, become the playground of the young prince. There he discovers the simple pleasures of childhood, chasing after the birds with iridescent feathers and marveling at the fish that shimmer like living jewels in the sacred pools. It is a world of wonders, where every stone and every plant seem imbued with magic and ancient stories.

But beyond the walls of the palace, Egypt is murmuring with concerns. The ancient gods, once neglected for the sole worship of Aten, are beginning to demand their due, and the priests of Thebes, guardians of the immemorial traditions, observe the child with hope and calculation. They see in him the potential for a return to the cosmic order, a way to restore the balance between the world of the living and that of the deities.

Tutankhamun, still unconscious of the power games going on around him, grows up in the gentle breezes of the Nile and the warmth of a benevolent sun. The teachings he receives are steeped in ancient wisdom and deep knowledge, preparing his mind for the complexity of future responsibilities. The stars themselves seem to watch over his sleep, weaving in the sky the destiny of a king who one day will have to guide Egypt through the twists and turns of history.

Thus, in the secret of the royal chambers and the quiet of the gardens, the first years of Tutankhamun pass, like the waters of the Nile nourishing the fertile earth. And while the young prince learns about his world, Egypt waits, holding its breath, for the moment when he will emerge as Pharaoh, bearing the hopes and dreams of an eternal civilization.

In the palace corridors, where shadows dance to the flickering flames of torches, the young Tutankhamun grows under the weight of a complex legacy. The whispers of the past echo against the stone walls, constantly reminding the controversial figure of his predecessor, Akhenaten, whose Amarna revolution shook the established order.

The accounts of Akhenaten's revolution, with its radical ideals and exclusive worship of the solar disk Aten, permeate the atmosphere with a palpable tension. The priests, once sidelined, exchange meaningful looks, while the servants whisper stories about the days when the temples were closed and the ancient gods were renounced.

Tutankhamun, whose very name is a tribute to the god Amun rehabilitated, is raised in the shadow of the revolution that divided his people. The brightly colored frescoes of the Amarna period, with their bold and naturalistic representations, contrast with the traditional images of the gods and goddesses with idealized forms. It is a visual world that is fighting for its identity, a testimony to the struggle between the old and the new.

The young prince witnesses the restoration of ancient cults, an attempt to heal the wounds left by his father's radical changes. Statues of Aten are replaced by those of Amun and other deities, and hymns to the glory of the sun give way to the age-old prayers whispered in reopened temples.

In the gardens of the palace, where the statues of Akhenaten and his family have been defaced or overturned, Tutankhamun plays among the remains of a bygone era. He is educated by tutors who teach him to venerate the traditional gods, but also to understand the complexity of his father's faith. It is a lesson in balance between respect for tradition and recognition of the mistakes of the past.

As the sun sets, tinting the sky with shades of gold and purple, Tutankhamun stands on a balcony, contemplating the Nile. He is the product of two worlds, one long gone and the other rising from its ashes. And in the silence of the night that falls, he wonders what kind of king he will become. Will he be the shadow of his father, or the light that will lead Egypt to a future reconciled with its glorious past? Only time, this eternal scribe of history, can carve the answer into the stone of destiny.

Egypt, the cradle of ancient civilizations, saw the birth and growth of monarchs whose names resonate through the ages. Among them, a child-king, Tutankhamun, whose destiny was as short as it was dazzling, like a shooting star in the night sky of the Nile.

In the royal apartments, where the scents of incense mix with the essences of lotus, the young Tutankhamun is surrounded by tutors and advisers. They oversee his education, instilling in him the secrets of power and the subtleties of

Egyptian religion. Each day is a lesson, each gesture an apprenticeship for one who is destined to be more than a man: a pharaoh, a living god in the eyes of his people.

The games of childhood give way to military exercises and philosophical debates. The models of tanks and ivory figurines of soldiers are not simple toys, but learning tools to understand the art of war and the management of an empire. The walls of the palace, adorned with frescoes depicting legendary battles, are the silent witnesses of his preparation for royalty.

Beyond formal learning, it is in the heart and mind of the young king that the true preparation takes place. He learns to listen to the murmurings of the people, to understand the needs of the temples and the priests, to balance justice and mercy. The gods themselves seem to whisper advice in his ear, through the hot winds that blow on the sacred shores of the river.

As the moon rises in the sky, illuminating the columns of the Karnak temple, Tutankhamun, dressed in fine linen and sparkling jewelry, stands in front of the altar. The priests sing sacred songs, and the people bow before their sovereign. He is young, certainly, but already he bears on his shoulders the weight of a gold crown, symbol of his power over the Two Lands.

In the silence of the night, while the stars watch over eternal Egypt, the child-king makes a promise to the gods and to himself: he will be a just pharaoh, a protector of his people, a builder of monuments that will defy time. And in this vow, there is the determination of a king who, despite his young age, understands the scope of his inheritance and the fragility of his reign.

The early ascension of Tutankhamun to the throne of Egypt is an event shrouded in mystery and destiny. The young prince, barely out of childhood, is suddenly thrust into the heart of palace intrigues and power games that define the apex of the divine and earthly hierarchy of ancient Egypt.

The tributes are presented by official representatives of the neighboring countries as well as dignitaries of the kingdom.

"O Tutankhamun, king of light, ...
>Our beloved Pharaoh,
>We pay tribute to you with respect and admiration
>And we worship you as a god on earth.

>You are our guide and protector
>And we are proud to serve you and follow you,
>You reign with wisdom and goodness
>And you are a just and beloved Pharaoh of your people.

>We offer you these gifts, oh king
>In a sign of our respect and loyalty
>And we pray that you reign over our country
>With wisdom and prosperity, for eternity.

>May the gods protect and bless you
>O Tutankhamun, king of light."

In the palace corridors, where shadows dance in the torchlight, the counselors murmur about the sudden passage of the young prince with the stature of a pharaoh. The priests, nobles, and scribes observe with curiosity tinged with apprehension this change of guard, this shifting of the stars that places a child at the top of the most powerful civilization in the known world.

The coronation ceremony is a spectacle of grandeur and solemnity. Temples fill with the sweet smell of burning kyphi, and chants rise to the celestial vaults, as if to touch the gods themselves. Tutankhamun, dressed in the ceremonial clothes of the pharaoh, receives the insignia of his power: the heqa scepter and the nekhekh whip, symbols of his authority over life and death.

The people's eyes are riveted on this young king, whose head is crowned with the striped nemes of gold and the uraeus, the protective cobra. He advances towards the throne, his steps echoing on the stone slabs, each movement scrutinized by the assembly. He finally sits down, and silence falls, a silence heavy with promises and expectations.

In this moment, Tutankhamun is no longer a child. He is the living embodiment of Horus, the celestial falcon, the link between the gods and men. He is the guarantor of Ma'at, the cosmic order, the one who must maintain the balance between the forces of chaos and light. His youth is forgotten, replaced by the majesty of his charge.

And as the sun rises, flooding the columns of the temple and the faces of the statues of the gods with light, Tutankhamun begins his reign. A reign that, although marked by brevity, will be immortalized in the annals of history, carved in stone and protected by the sands of the desert for eternity.

The influence of counselors and regents on the young Tutankhamun is a fascinating chapter of Egyptian history, where the invisible strings of power are pulled into the shadows by experienced and ambitious hands. In the halls of the palace, where each stone could tell a story of conspiracy or loyalty, the fate of Egypt is played out through the whispered advice of a child-king.

Ay, the wise and cunning advisor, is a fatherly figure and a political guide for Tutankhamun. His advice is steeped in the wisdom of the years and intimate knowledge of state affairs since the reign of Amenhotep III. He often stands next to the throne, his impassive face hiding the machinations of his mind that is constantly working to navigate the turbulent waters of Egyptian politics.

Horemheb, the powerful general, is the armed arm of the kingdom, the one who ensures the protection of the Pharaoh and the stability of the borders. His military exploits are legendary, and his presence at the court is a constant reminder of the force that underlies the reign of Tutankhamun. He is the wall against which the waves of the enemies of Egypt break, but also a potential rival for power.

In the background, other less known but equally influential figures weave the web of administration and daily management of the kingdom. The viziers, scribes and high-ranking priests form a complex network of relationships and influences, where each decision can have repercussions on the delicate balance of power.

The court is a theatre where a play with multiple acts is performed, and Tutankhamun, although Pharaoh, is sometimes more spectator than actor. The advisers and regents, with their ambitions and plans, partly shape the reign of the young king, guiding him through the rites of passage that will make him a sovereign in his own right.

But beyond the manipulations and strategies, there is a deep respect for the divinity embodied by Tutankhamun. The advisers, aware of their role as guardians of the throne of Horus, strive to preserve the majesty and continuity of the pharaonic line, even if it means acting on behalf of a king who has not yet reached the fullness of his power.

And so, in the palace's atmosphere of incense and whispers, the young Tutankhamun grew up, surrounded by men who were both his protectors, his mentors, and his greatest challenges.

The reconstruction of ties with the clergy of Amun, during the reign of Tutankhamun, is a period of reconciliation and spiritual renewal. After the upheaval of the Amarna Revolution, the young pharaoh finds himself at the crossroads of Egyptian history, where the fate of traditional religion is in his hands.

The young king, advised by experienced viziers and priests, undertakes to restore the ancient gods to their rightful place. Temples, once neglected in favor of the exclusive worship of Aten, are restored and embellished. Statues of Amun, hidden or mutilated during the reign of Akhenaten, are given back their place of honor with great ceremony.

Tutankhamun, although a puppet in the hands of his advisers, is the symbol of this restoration. He actively participates in rites and processions, renewing the ties between royalty and clergy. The priests of Amun, regaining their influence and power, orchestrate a return to the sources of Egyptian faith, where the pantheon of gods is once again venerated in all its diversity.

The royal decrees affirm Tutankhamun's desire to see the two powers of Egypt, the throne and the temple, work together. The donation of land and wealth to temples multiplies, ensuring the prosperity of the clergy and, by extension, that of Egypt itself.

In this transitional period, Tutankhamun reveals himself to be the bridge between two eras, the one who brought balance back to the land of the Two Kingdoms. The reintegration of traditional deities during his reign is seen not only as a restoration of the old order but also as an act of divine justice, repairing the fractures caused by the excesses of the past.

The Crown on a Child's Forehead

In the silent halls of the palace of Thebes, where the shadows of the ancestors murmured eternal advice, Tutankhamun, child-king crowned with the double crown of Upper and Lower Egypt, stood facing the horizon of his reign. His young shoulders bore the weight of an empire that had been shaken by the storms of the Amarna Revolution, and now he had to navigate the troubled waters of politics and religion.

Every day was a challenge, a mystery wrapped in the ties of royalty. The counselors, like hawks around their prey, whispered strategies and intrigues, trying to weave their ambitions into the fabric of power that the young pharaoh held in his inexperienced hands. Tutankhamun listened, learned, but in the secret of his heart, he dreamed of a reign that would be his, not the one dictated by the shadows that danced around his throne.

The young king was faced with the challenge of reconciling a people with their gods, of restoring the temples and rites that his predecessor had abandoned. He had to walk a tightrope between respect for tradition and the need to leave a personal mark on the sand of time. The priests of Amun watched him, hoping to see in him a champion of their cause, a restorer of the old ways.

But there was more. Tutankhamun had to guide Egypt through the twists and turns of international diplomacy, maintain the borders against the ambitions of the Hittites and other foreign peoples, and ensure the prosperity of a people who had known division and uncertainty.

And then there was the illness, the insidious shadow that lingered near his throne, threatening to cut short his dreams and ambitions. The doctors whispered, the magicians chanted, but destiny remained as unreadable as the hieroglyphs on the walls of the tombs of the kings. The pharaoh was physically diminished by a clubfoot as well as by the contraction of malaria.

In the solitude of his royal apartments, far from the curious eyes and indiscreet ears, Tutankhamun was allowed to remove his mask of sovereignty. There, in front of the images of his ancestors, he was simply a young man facing eternity, a pharaoh who was looking for his way in the labyrinth of history.

At sunrise, when the first golden rays touched the lotus-shaped columns of the great palace of Thebes, Tutankhamun, the living incarnation of the god Horus, emerged from his private quarters. The morning rituals began with purifying ablutions, the water of the Nile used to wash the sleep from his eyes like those of a falcon, and to prepare his mind for the divine tasks to come.

Dressed in fine linen, adorned with jewels that caught the light like stars captured, he was the very image of majesty. His priests and servants were busy around him, reciting prayers and incantations, making sure that every detail of his appearance was impeccable, worthy of a god among men.

The breakfast was a solemn affair, with offerings of bread, beer, meat and fruit being presented first to the gods, and then consumed by the pharaoh. Each bite was an act of communion with the divine, each gulp a blessing for the fertile land of Egypt.

Then came the time of the audiences. Seated on his golden throne, under the benevolent gaze of the vultures and the protective snakes, Tutankhamun listened to the reports of his viziers, the requests of his subjects, and rendered justice with the wisdom of an earthly Osiris. The ambassadors of distant lands bowed before his splendor, bringing gifts and treaties, seeking the favor of the young god-king.

The afternoon was dedicated to state affairs and inspections of ongoing work. In a chariot, he toured the streets of Thebes, greeting the population who prostrated themselves as he passed, or visited the construction sites of temples and tombs, making sure that each stone was a hymn to longevity.

But even a god needed a break. In the private gardens of the palace, where lotuses bloomed and birds sang, Tutankhamun could retreat for a moment of contemplation. There, he meditated on the mysteries of Aten and Amun, seeking balance between light and shadow, between heaven and earth.

The evening was falling, and with it, the bedtime rituals began. Incense and myrrh burned in the braziers, filling the air with scents that led the divine king to the world of dreams. Before retiring to the quiet of his apartments, Tutankhamun stood for a moment at the window of the apparition, blessing his people with a gesture of the hand, a fleeting pharaoh under the eternal stars.

In the silence of the night, alone with his thoughts, the young divine king closed his eyes, knowing that each day was a gift from the gods, each night a journey into the afterlife. And in those dark hours, perhaps he dreamed of a world where he would be free to run, laugh and love like any other boy his age, far from the crown and the scepter, far from the watchful eye of the gods.

The Shadows of Power

The faint light of dawn creeps through the palace columns as the young king's counselors, like ghosts, gather for a secret meeting. They murmur, plot, and devise plans to guide, and sometimes even manipulate, the child sovereign whose crown weighs heavily on a head still full of youthful dreams.

In the shadow of these powerful men, Tutankhamun grows, learns, and changes. He listens, observes, and sometimes, in the privacy of his chambers, he lets out a sigh of frustration. For if the gods made him king, the men made him a puppet.

But not all shadows are enemies. There are also those that protect, that teach, that love. Among them is Ankhesenamun, his young wife, whose eyes shine with a light that belongs only to her. She is the whisper of truth in a world of lies, the gentle hand in the lonely night, the promise of a future where perhaps, the shadows will dissipate to make way for the light of a true reign.

For the moment, Tutankhamun walks through a labyrinth whose every wall is a secret, every door an enigma. But the Ariadne's thread is there, in the pure heart of a king who, despite the shadows, seeks the light.

Ai, the wisest of the wise, is a man whose life has been woven in the golden threads of power. He is the advisor, the mentor, the one who whispers in the ear of kings and who, with his parchment hands, shapes the future of Egypt. In the veins of this old vizier flows the ink of royal decrees, and his mind is a papyrus on which is written the destiny of the nation.

Horemheb, on the other hand, is the warrior shadow, the protector of the empire. His stature is that of a colossal statue at the entrance of a temple, intimidating and reassuring at the same time. He is the shield against enemies, the sharp sword in the darkness of uncertainty. His gaze is a challenge, his step a warning; he is the iron hand in the velvet glove of power.

Together, these two men form an almost mythical duo, the guardians of a kingdom that stands at the crossroads. Ay, with his political machinations, weaves the web of the future, while Horemheb, with his brute force, ensures that Egypt will not falter under the weight of external threats.

But behind their apparent devotion are ambitions that know no bounds. Ay, the man in the shadows, aspires to a light that is not meant for him, while Horemheb, the warrior, dreams of laurels that are not yet within his reach. They are the figures in the shadows, the puppeteers whose strings are intertwined in a dance of power that one day might well escape their control.

Tutankhamun, young pharaoh with clear eyes, is the most precious puppet in their hands. He is the symbol of a golden age that both seek to shape according to their vision. But the young king's heart beats with independence that could, in the end, undo the tightest knots of this palace intrigue.

In the game of shadows and light that is played in the corridors of power, Ay and Horemheb are unavoidable figures, pillars on which the throne of Egypt rests. But even the most solid pillars can erode under the wind of change, and in the eyes of Tutankhamun is read a promise of renewal that could well redraw the map of power in this land of the pharaohs.

In the secret alcoves of the palace of Thebes, the murmurs are as sharp as the blades of swords. The corridors echo with the sounds of conspiracies hatched in the shadows, where the ambitions of men collide and intertwine like the snakes of the desert. It is a world where trust is as rare as pure gold and where every smile conceals a hidden intention.

Tutankhamun, young and carefree, is the lighthouse around which the conspirators revolve. His innocence is a diaphanous veil that the shrewdest seek to pierced to infuse their designs. Ay, the vizier, is a master in the art of manipulation, a puppeteer whose agile fingers pull the strings of power with an ability that borders on divinity. Horemheb, the general, is the armed wing of this invisible force, ready to strike where the vizier directs.

The nobles and the priests observe, calculate, and plot their own plans. Each aspires to a share of the royal cake, to a fragment of the immense power that emanates from the golden throne. They are like vultures hovering above a feast, waiting for the right moment to swoop down on their prey.

In this arena where the destiny of a nation is played out, alliances are made and broken to the beat of the young king's heart. Promises are as volatile as the sands of the desert, and oaths as ephemeral as the lotus flowers. The priests of Amun, long overshadowed by the solar cult of Aten, weave in silence the web of their return, infusing in the mind of the young pharaoh the seeds of a glorious past that could well be the key to their ascent.

In this dance of death, Tutankhamun is both the judge and the prize, the symbol of a bygone era and the promise of a future to be rebuilt. The power struggles taking place in the shadows of his reign are as complex as the hieroglyphs that adorn the walls of the temples, and just as indestructible.

The fate of Egypt hangs by a thread as thin as a spider's web, woven between the pillars of truth and deception. In this labyrinth of lies and half-truths, the young Tutankhamun will have to find his way, guided by the light of wisdom that, it is hoped, will be granted to him by the gods themselves.

In the fertile valley of the Nile, under the eternal azure of a cloudless sky, the young Tutankhamun, Pharaoh of the land of Egypt, strives to engrave his name in the stone of history. Each day that passes is a new page on which he records the acts of his reign, under the scrutinizing gaze of the gods and men.

The royal palace is abuzz with activity, like a beehive where every servant, every advisor, every priest plays their role in the great symphony of power. The young king, adorned with the decorations associated with his position, is the living embodiment of Maat , the principle of truth and order on which the universe rests. His decisions, whether it be to decree a law, to launch a commercial expedition, or to order the construction of a temple, are all stones laid on the path to his eternity.

With a pen dipped in the ink of wisdom, he signs decrees that resonate across the two lands of Egypt. He orders the restoration of temples abandoned during the Amarna period, thus reconnecting with ancient traditions and appeasing the clergy of Amun. He sends his armies to pacify distant lands, ensuring the security of his empire's borders. He inaugurates irrigation projects that transform arid lands into fertile gardens, winning the hearts of his people with these acts of benevolence.

But the acts of a king are not all inscribed in stone or proclaimed in the courts. Some are whispered in the intimacy of the royal apartments, where the young Tutankhamun, far from the eyes, turns out to be a man with dreams and desires, a sovereign who loves, who doubts, who hopes. There, in the secret of his thoughts, he dreams of a prosperous and peaceful kingdom, of a happy people and of an assured posterity.

The actions of a king are the mirror of his soul, and Tutankhamun, despite his youth and the shadows that loom over his reign, aspires to reflect the light of a just and benevolent sovereign. His actions, whether great or small, are the golden threads woven into the great tapestry of time, threads that, he hopes, will form the image of a golden reign in the annals of Egyptian history.

Ankhesenamun: The Companion of a Royal Destiny

In the meanders of the palace of gold and azure, where the scents of lotus mix with the smells of incense, Ankhesenamun, the great royal wife, walks with the grace of a goddess among mortals. Her silhouette, as elegant as the papyrus columns that support the vast halls of the palace, is a vision of beauty and majesty that inspires both love and respect.

Daughter of Akhenaten and Nefertiti, she carries within her the legacy of a religious revolution and an aesthetic that shook Egypt. But it is at the side of Tutankhamun, her husband and half-brother, that she finds her true vocation: to be the pillar on which the young king can lean, the confidante who shares his dreams and concerns, the queen who must ensure the continuity of the royal line.

In the intimacy of their apartments, far from indiscreet ears, they exchange sweet words, plans for the future, and hopes for a prosperous reign. Ankhesenamun, with her wisdom and intelligence, is often the voice of reason that guides Tutankhamun through the complex labyrinth of governance. She is also the tender companion who, in the silence of the night, knows how to soothe the fears of a king confronted with the weight of his crown.

Their union, sealed by the gods and celebrated by men, is a symbol of stability in a kingdom still haunted by the ghosts of Amarna. Together, they participate in the great religious ceremonies, reinforcing by their presence the link between the throne and the divine. Ankhesenamun, as Great Royal Wife, plays a crucial role in these rituals, where her figure is venerated as the earthly incarnation of Hathor, goddess of love and motherhood.

But fate is often unpredictable, and the life of Ankhesenamun is marked by shadows of tragedy. The loss of their children, whose small forms rest in the canopic jars, is a wound that does not close, a grief that even the most fervent prayers cannot ease. Yet in these moments of pain, the bond between the pharaoh and his queen strengthens, forging between them a complicity that transcends the trials.

Ankhesenamun, in the great theater of Egyptian history, plays her role with dignity and strength that commands admiration. Her life, woven with joys and sorrows, is a reflection of an era of change, of a kingdom trying to reinvent itself after the turmoil of the past. And in the heart of Tutankhamun, she is and will forever be the companion of a royal destiny, the other half of a soul that aspires to immortality under the eternal stars of the Egyptian sky.

Between War and Diplomacy: The Horizons of Tutankhamun

Tutankhamun, heir to an empire whose borders extend beyond the visible horizon, finds himself facing a world in full effervescence. The drums of war resound at the limits of his kingdom, while diplomatic missives pile up in the halls of the council, bearing the seals of distant kingdoms and vassal city-states.

The young pharaoh, although trained in the arts of peace and diplomacy, understands that the stability of his empire rests on the strength of his armies and the wisdom of his alliances. Under the weight of the double crown of Egypt, he orders campaigns to reaffirm his sovereignty over the contested lands, where the Egyptian chariots, as fast as the wind of the desert, make the deserters and rebels tremble.

The generals, veterans of battles under the reign of Akhenaten, stand ready to carry out the orders of their divine king. They share with him the strategies of war, the detailed maps of the disputed territories, and the stories of past exploits. Tutankhamun, despite his youth, shows a keen understanding of military issues and the ability to inspire his troops, who see in him not only a sovereign, but a promising leader of war.

In parallel, the young king engages in a refined diplomatic dance, where each ambassador is received with the honors due to his land. The sumptuous banquets, where exotic dishes and wines aged in the royal cellars are served, are opportunities to forge bonds of friendship and seal pacts. The sumptuous gifts exchanged between courts are the mute witnesses of these agreements, and the foreign princesses, arriving in a procession to marry the Egyptian princes, are the living proof of lasting peace.

But the diplomacy of Tutankhamun is not only a matter of pomp and ceremony. In the secret of the hushed rooms, far from indiscreet eyes, he listens attentively to the advice of his viziers, weighing each word, each proposal, with a maturity that exceeds his age. He knows that each treaty signed, each alliance forged, is a step closer to the prosperity of his people and the perpetuity of his reign.

The military campaigns and foreign relations, under the reign of Tutankhamun, are thus the expression of a balanced policy, where force and wisdom are combined to ensure the greatness of Egypt. And if the gods are with him, if the luck of the righteous accompanies him, then his name will be inscribed on the steles of victory and in the annals of the people, as that of a pharaoh who knew, with the vigor of youth and the intelligence of the sage, to navigate the tumultuous waters of his time.

The Fragility of a Pharaoh: The Trials of Tutankhamun

In the secret chambers of the palace, where the whispers of the servants are lost in the echoes of the long corridors, the health of the young Tutankhamun is the subject of all attention and all concern. The Pharaoh, incarnate deity in the eyes of his people, bears the marks of fragile humanity, marked by insidious diseases and disabilities that constrain him in his simplest movements.

The royal doctors, guardians of ancient knowledge and remedies inherited from the gods, busy themselves around their sovereign with ointments and potions, seeking to alleviate his suffering. They scrutinize the signs and symptoms, read in the entrails of sacrificed animals and consult the stars, hoping to find the foreshadowing of a cure or divine will.

Tutankhamun, although afflicted by these ills, does not let himself be overcome. His mind, quick and determined, rises above the limitations of his body. He finds in art, music, and poetry, refuges where his soul can express itself freely, far from physical constraints. The frescoes in his palace, painted with a grace and delicacy that defy the sturdiness of the stones, are a mirror of his inner world, rich and unaltered.

The pharaoh's disabilities are not only a personal challenge; they are also a political issue. Courtiers and dignitaries observe, some with compassion, others with cold calculation, how their king faces his trials. Alliances are made and broken in the shadow of his faltering health, and priests murmur prayers for the strength of their living god, knowing that the stability of the kingdom is intimately linked to the strength of its monarch.

Despite this, Tutankhamun appears to his people during great ceremonies, supported by finely crafted canes, symbols of both his weakness and his resilience. He appears in his golden chariot, pulled by spirited horses, as if to defy the evils that assail him. And the people, seeing in him the strength of a young tree that bends but does not break under the wind, love him all the more for his courage and perseverance.

In the annals of history, the health of Tutankhamun, with his diseases and disabilities, will become the subject of many speculation and studies. But beyond the analysis and theories, what will remain engraved in the collective memory is the image of a king who, in the face of adversity, was able to keep his head high, govern with wisdom and inspire his people with his indomitable bravery.

Between Shadow and Light: The Confrontation of Tutankhamun and Ay

At the dawn of his nineteenth year, Tutankhamun, the child-king become a symbol of the resurgence of traditions, stands at the crossroads of his destiny. The walls of the palace, silent witnesses of the power struggles, echo with the sounds of an increasing tension between the young pharaoh and Ay, the eminent counselor, paternalistic figure and architect of the shadow.

Ay, Akhenaten's former right-hand man and regent of the kingdom during the minority of Tutankhamun, had long manipulated the strings of power with an skill that bordered on art. But with a Tutankhamun coming of age, roles and influences are called into question. The pharaoh, once docile, transforms into a sovereign with strong ideas, refusing to bow to the will of the one who had guided him.

The decision that ignites passions and marks the beginning of an era of discord is a royal decree, a proclamation that was supposed to seal the kingdom's future. Ay, with the subtlety of a chess player, had counted on an unresisting signature, a formality like so many others. But Tutankhamun, enlightened by the advice of his own allies, sees in it a hindrance to his sovereignty, a trap woven in the shadows to keep him under tutelage.

The pharaoh's refusal causes ripples that spread through the corridors of power. The murmurs become more insistent, the looks more loaded with innuendo. Ay, whose cold anger is as formidable as the burning sands of the desert, sees his influence threatened. He cannot tolerate this affront from a young king who, in his eyes, should still be listening to his elders.

The counselors are divided, some remaining faithful to Ay, others joining the cause of a Tutankhamun who wishes to record his reign in history, not as the epilogue of a bygone era, but as the prologue of a new era. The stormy debates extend even to the throne rooms, where the arguments clash with the force of the Nile storms.

Tutankhamun, in an act of defiance that echoes like the sound of a gong, makes decisions that affirm his independence. He orders construction, launches reforms, and above all, surrounds himself with loyalists who share his vision of a renewed Egypt. Ay, on the other hand, is not a man to retreat into the shadows without reacting. He hatches plans, forges alliances, preparing the ground for a possible reclamation of his lost influence.

The confrontation between Tutankhamun and Ay is not only a conflict of wills; it is a reflection of a greater struggle between the past and the future, between the remnants of an old order and the promises of a renewal. And as the sun sets over Thebes, the city of a hundred gates, the two figures, young king and old advisor, stand face to face, each carrying a vision for Egypt, each determined to see his dream become reality.

In the sacred enclosure of the palace of Thebes, where destinies are woven and undone, the tension between Tutankhamun and Ay had reached its apogee. The walls, impregnated with the history of the pharaohs, were going to be the silent witnesses of a drama that would forever mark ancient Egypt.

The frustration of the young Tutankhamun, exacerbated by the incessant conflicts with Ay, was boiling like the tumultuous waters of the Nile in flood. The counselor, once mentor and guide, had become the embodiment of an authority that the pharaoh could no longer tolerate. The exchanges between the two men, once filled with respect, had turned into verbal confrontations charged with corrosive bitterness.

In a fateful encounter, the words were replaced by a gesture of unparalleled violence. Ay, carried away by a smoldering anger, seized the cane of Tutankhamun, symbol of his royal power, and, in a surge of fury, struck the pharaoh on the left temple. The blow, of brute force, made the young king stagger. Tutankhamun staggered, his frail and sickly body unable to withstand the violence of the assault. He fell and his tibia broke in his fall as unconsciousness enveloped him like a shroud.

The hours that followed were filled with desperate urgency. The servants and priests bustled about, powerless, while the Great Royal Wife, Ankhsenamun, approached her husband. The murmur of the incantations mixed with the silent prayers, in the hope of a vain miracle.

Tutankhamun, the child pharaoh, the divine king, lay there, his breath of life unraveling like the last rays of the sun disappearing on the horizon. Ankesenamun, in a mix of pain and devotion, held her husband's hand, accompanying him in his final moments. Her eyes, filled with tears, reflected the flickering light of the torches, witnesses to the end of an era.

The silence descended on the royal chamber when the last breath of Tutankhamun escaped from his lips. The Great Royal Wife, who remained at his side, placed one last kiss on the forehead of her beloved, thus sealing their eternal goodbye. The reign of Tutankhamun, bearer of so many hopes and dreams of renewal, ended with a murmur, leaving behind a shaken kingdom and an uncertain future.

And as news of the tragedy spread like a dark wind through the palace colonnades, Egypt mourned its lost pharaoh, its child-king whose life had been cut down by the hand of the one who had sworn to protect him.

The Precipitous Farewells and the Call to the Distant

Hardly had the last breath of Tutankhamun dissipated in the incense-laden air of the palace when Ay, in a pragmatic surge tinged with ambition, was already busy organizing the funeral of the young pharaoh. The rites, usually solemn and spread over long periods to honor the gods and prepare the deceased for his journey to the afterlife, were accelerated with indecent haste.

Ay, whose soul was already turned towards his own advent, made a decision that would mark the history of Egypt with a shadow of scandal. He appropriated the majestic tomb that Tutankhamun had built, an eternal dwelling worthy of a Pharaoh, and relegated the body of his predecessor to a more modest tomb, an eternal rest that in no way reflected the greatness of his lineage.

At the same time, Ay, thirsty for power, turned his eyes towards Ankhesenamun, the grieving widow. He coveted not only the legitimacy that his marriage to the Great Royal Wife would confer upon him, but also the ascension to the throne that would result from it. He pressed the young queen to marry him, a proposal that sounded more like an order than a marriage proposal.

Ankhesenamun, the great royal wife of the deceased Pharaoh Tutankhamun, was in a desperate situation. Ay, the ambitious vizier, coveted the throne of Egypt and saw in her the means to establish his legitimacy as Pharaoh. He was not of royal blood, and without her by his side, his claims to the throne would be in vain. The young widow, however, refused to submit to a forced marriage with one she considered an usurper.

In a bold act of defiance, she made the decision to address Suppiluliuma I, the powerful king of the Hittites, sworn enemies of Egypt. She sent him a letter, a cry for help engraved on a clay tablet, in the hope of finding an ally and a royal husband to maintain her status and protect her country.

The letter, written in Akkadian cuneiform, the diplomatic language of the time, was a poignant appeal:

"My husband died and I don't have a son. They say you have a lot of sons. You could give me one of your sons to become my husband. I wouldn't want to take one of my subjects as a husband... I'm afraid!

Suppiluliuma I, initially skeptical, thought first of a ruse. But faced with the insistence of Ankhesenamun, who sent him a second even more imploring message, he finally gave in. Zannanza, his third son, was chosen to become the pharaoh of Egypt and the husband of the queen in distress.

However, fate decided otherwise. Before the Hittite prince could even set foot on Egyptian soil, war broke out. Zannanza's body was sent back to his father, killed under mysterious circumstances.

The assassination of Zannanza sparked a major diplomatic incident. Letters full of anger and accusations were exchanged between the two empires. Tension rose until Hittite forces launched attacks against Egyptian colonies in Syria, leading to open war.

Zannanza, although he never reigned, remains a tragic figure in Egyptian history. His premature death symbolizes the power struggles and political maneuvering of the time, a dangerous game where conspirators would stop at nothing to prevent a foreign king from ascending the throne of Egypt.

In the palace's hushed corridors, where the murmurings of conspiracies mixed with the priests' chants, Ay, the usurper, was hatching his final scheme. The arrival of the Hittite prince Zannanza, sent in response to the desperate call of Ankhesenamun, should have marked the beginning of a new era for Egypt. But Ay, consumed by a thirst for power, could not tolerate such an outcome.

With the complicity of Horemheb, an ruthless general and menacing shadow behind the throne, Ay orchestrated the assassination of the foreign prince. Zannanza, who crossed mountains and deserts bearing hopes of peace, met his death in a cowardly ambush, far from his homeland, his blood mixing with the burning sand that was supposed to be his salvation.

The news of this tragedy plunged Ankhesenamun into an abyss of desolation. She, who had dared to dream of an escape, saw herself forced to accept the hand of the usurper. Ay, in an act of brutal domination, married the Great Royal Wife, thus sealing his ascent to the rank of Pharaoh. The ceremony, devoid of any affection or reverence, was a bitter spectacle for the gods and men.

Ay, now pharaoh, reigned with an iron fist, imposing his will on a court that feared him more than it respected him. Rumors of his violence and conspiracies spread like a bad wind, poisoning the atmosphere of the Nile Valley. Egypt, once a land of majesty and sacred mysteries, now seemed caught in the grip of an uncertain future.

Ankhesenamun, reduced to silence, was nothing more than a shadow of herself, a queen without a kingdom, a widow without tears, a prisoner of a marriage that was a chain more than a sacred bond. Her gaze, once filled with the light of the stars, now only reflected the emptiness of the infinite desert.

Thus ended an era, not with the grandeur of the ancient pharaohs, but in the muffled tumult of betrayals and disproportionate ambitions. Egypt, waiting for better days, turned the page of Amarna, leaving behind the broken dreams of a divine revolution and the hopes of a princess who had dared to defy destiny.

The Erasure of a Dynasty

The reign of Ay was as brief as it was stormy, a shooting star in the eternal sky of Egypt, extinguished as quickly as it had shone. His sudden disappearance left the throne at the mercy of Horemheb, the iron general, whose ambitions knew no bounds.

Horemheb, once crowned, embarked on a merciless campaign to erase all traces of his predecessors from Egyptian memory. The monuments of Akhenaten, the inscriptions of Tutankhamun, and even the remains of Ay were hammered, scraped, and destroyed with almost religious fervor. Statues were toppled, the names of heretical pharaohs were banned from the annals, and their tombs were desecrated in a posthumous act of revenge.

The new pharaoh was relentless in restoring ancient order, renewing ties with the clergy of Amun and reaffirming traditional cults. The temples of Aten were closed, their priests dispersed, and the faithful were forced to renounce their faith or practice it in secret, under threat of reprisal.

Horemheb, who was not of royal blood, positioned himself as the restorer of Egypt's greatness, but his reign was marked by an atmosphere of suspicion and fear. Courtiers whispered in the shadows, fearing that their name would be next on the pharaoh's list of enemies. repression was everywhere, and personal security was only assured by unconditional loyalty to the throne.

Under Horemheb, Egypt seemed to return to a surface stability, but the beating heart of its culture had been altered. The 18th dynasty, once the height of power and innovation, ended in a climate of revisionism and repression. The end of this era not only marked the closure of a tumultuous chapter of

Egyptian history, but also the advent of a new era, where the shadows of the past would be forever buried under the sand of time.

The Eternity of a Name

In the quicksand of history, where empires rise and fall with the regularity of tides, ancient Egypt has always managed to preserve its mystery and grandeur. Horemheb, the last sovereign of the 18th dynasty, tried to rewrite history, to erase the names of those he considered heretics and usurpers. But the irony of destiny wanted that, in his quest for forgetfulness, he inadvertently paved the way to immortality for the youngest of them, Tutankhamun.

The name of Tutankhamun, which Horemheb sought to erase from the annals of history, has crossed millennia, eclipsing those of his contemporaries and even his persecutors. It is in the silence of his inviolate tomb, a sanctuary preserved by time and forgetfulness, that the young pharaoh reached eternity. When Howard Carter unveiled his sealed sarcophagus in 1922, he awakened the memory of a forgotten king, whose golden face became a symbol of eternal Egypt.

The ancient belief that repeating a name confers immortality upon its bearer has proven prophetic. Tutankhamun, the "boy pharaoh," achieved eternity not through the exploits of his reign, but through the fascination he inspired. His name is whispered by the lips of millions of people, echoing through the exhibitions, books, and stories that celebrate him.

In his attempt to erase Tutankhamun from history, Horemheb inadvertently strengthened his legend. Where he sought silence, he generated an echo that continues to amplify. Where he sought darkness, he lit a flame that shines through the ages. In the end, it is Tutankhamun who achieved what all pharaohs desired: a life after death, not in the fields of Ialou, but in the collective memory of humanity.

Thus, the young king, once erased, now reigns forever, not only in the afterlife promised by the ancient Egyptians, but also in the heart and mind of every person who pronounces his name. It is there, in the invocation of his memory, that Tutankhamun has truly achieved immortality.

Tutankhamun became the most famous of the pharaohs and achieved the ultimate goal that his name be spoken constantly in order to achieve eternal life. Tutankhamun, Tutankhamun, Tutankhamun the whole world pronounces the name of Tutankhamun for eternity.

CHAPTER V. EPILOGUE

CONCLUSION

In the pages of this narrative, we have traversed an fascinating path through the history of the 18th Egyptian dynasty, a period rich in events and characters who continue to fascinate and inspire. Our journey through this ancient time, told in a romanticized way, has brought to life historical figures and illuminated aspects of their reign that remain shrouded in mystery.

This theory, presented with a touch of fiction, offers an unprecedented perspective on historical facts and mysteries that, to this day, remain unresolved. It opens a window into a world where history and fiction mix, thus offering an alternative vision of the events that shaped this crucial period in Egyptian history.

According to this interpretation, Neferneferuaten Tasherit would have taken over from Akhenaten. Tutankhamun, seen here as the son of Akhenaten and Beketaten (also probably known as the Younger Lady), would have inherited the throne in a complex and intriguing succession. This narration also suggests that Moses could be identified as Prince Thutmose, the brother of Akhenaten, thus laying the foundations for the great monotheistic religions that emerged later. And to conclude, it is suggested that it was Ay who orchestrated the tragic end of Tutankhamun. In a final act of greed and manipulation, Ay not only seized the tomb intended for the young pharaoh, but also his wife Ankhesenamun, the Great Royal Wife of Tutankhamun, in the ultimate goal of sitting himself on the throne of Egypt. All the more so since Ay had his tomb built in Amarna city which was abandoned after the death of Akhenaten, and he found himself at the twilight of his life without his own tomb. This action, marked by opportunism and betrayal, reveals the dark intrigues that were playing out behind the scenes of power in ancient Egypt. It is also conjectured that the tomb of Tutankhamun was not originally intended for him and that it could house an unexplored secret room, perhaps that of Neferneferuaten Tasherit or Meritaten.

These hypotheses, although lacking in tangible historical evidence at this stage, are the result of deep reflection and careful analysis. They represent a personal conviction, born of intuition and a deep understanding of this historical period. They invite reflection on the way in which events of the past can be interpreted and understood, and on the lasting impact they have on our understanding of the ancient world.

In short, this conclusion does not aim to establish indisputable historical facts, but rather to stimulate the imagination and encourage a deeper exploration of the mysteries of ancient Egypt. It is an invitation to consider the multiple facets of history, where facts mix with legends, and where each discovery can open the door to new interpretations and understandings.

CHAPTER VI. ANNEXES

CHRONOLOGY OF EVENTS

The chronology of events in ancient Egypt, particularly during the New Kingdom period, is crucial to understanding the complex and fascinating history of this civilization. Here is a structured overview of the key moments, centered around the reigns of Amenhotep III, Akhenaten, Tutankhamun and their successors, up to the time of Horemheb.

Amenhotep III: The Empire's High Point

Amenhotep III's reign (c. 1386-1349 BCE): A period of prosperity, stability, and artistic greatness. Amenhotep III extends Egyptian influence and beautifies the country with monumental construction.

Akhenaten and the Amarna Revolution

The reign of Akhenaten (around 1353 BC): Initially known as Amenhotep IV, he established the monotheistic cult of Aten.

Construction of Amarna (around 1346 BC): Akhenaten founded the city of Akhetaten (Amarna) as the center of his new cult.

Death of Akhenaten (around 1336 BC): His reign ends in controversy and uncertainty.

The Transition and the Reign of Tutankhamun

Reign of Neferneferuaten Tasherit (ca. 1336-1332 BCE): Period of transition and restoration of the ancient gods.

Tutankhamun's reign (c. 1332-1323 BC): The restoration of the cult of Amun and the return to Thebes. A reign marked by efforts to restore order and tradition.

Death of Tutankhamun (around 1323 BC): Death in mysterious circumstances, followed by the seizure of power by Ay.

The End of the New Empire

Reign of Ay (around 1323 to 1319 BC): Short period of reign, marked by the consolidation of power and marriage to Ankhesenamun.

Horemheb's reign (c. 1319 to 1292 BC): The last pharaoh of the 18th dynasty, Horemheb restored order and prepared the way for the 19th dynasty.

Epilogue and Legacy

The discovery of Tutankhamun's tomb in 1922. A discovery that shed light on the wealth of ancient Egypt and renewed global interest in its history.

The history of ancient Egypt is full of iconic figures whose lives and actions shaped not only their era but also the way we perceive this civilization today. Here is a snapshot of the key characters of this period, with a focus on the mysteries and intrigues that surround them.

Amenhotep III: The Magnificent

Amenhotep III: Pharaoh of grandeur and prosperity, known for his monumental constructions and peaceful reign. His marriage to Queen Tiyi, a woman of non-royal ascent, and his role in the preparation of the religious revolution of Akhenaten remain subjects of fascination.

Akhenaten: The Heretical Pharaoh

Akhenaten: Controversial figure, famous for replacing traditional polytheism with the monotheistic worship of Aten. The reasons behind this religious revolution, as well as the details of his personal life and death, are the subject of many debates and theories.

Thutmose/Moses: The Exodus to the Unknown

Thutmose/Moses: According to the theory, brother of Akhenaten and key figure of the biblical Exodus. His role as Minister of Cults and his choice to leave Egypt with the followers of Aten are crucial elements to understanding the links between Egyptian and biblical history.

Nefertiti and the Royal Family

Nefertiti: Akhenaten's chief wife, known for her beauty and influence. The circumstances of her disappearance are unresolved mysteries.

Meritaten and Neferneferuaten

Meritaten and Neferneferuaten Tasherit: Daughters of Akhenaten and Nefertiti, playing key roles in the post-Amarnian transition. Their influence and their marriages are key points to understand the dynasty. Their tombs remain to be found; would it be behind the tomb of Tutankhamun?

Tutankhamun: The Forgotten Pharaoh

Tutankhamun: Young pharaoh whose reign marked the return to ancient deities. The circumstances of his premature death and theories surrounding a possible assassination by Ay add a layer of mystery to his story.

Beketaten (Younger Lady)

Beketaten: Sister of Akhenaten, would she also be the mother and aunt of Tutankhamun?

Ay and Horemheb: The Successors

Ay: Successor and possible murderer of Tutankhamun, his reign is marked by intrigues and maneuvers to consolidate power.

Horemheb: Last pharaoh of the 18th dynasty, known for his efforts to restore order and erase the Amarna period.

Ancient Egypt was a civilization rich in beliefs and cultural practices, centered around fundamental concepts that formed the basis of their understanding of the world and the beyond. Here are some of these essential concepts.

Maat: The Cosmic Order

Representing justice, balance, and truth, Maat was considered the force governing the universe. Pharaohs were often seen as the guardians of Maat, responsible for maintaining order and stability in the kingdom. In everyday life as well as in the management of the state, respecting Maat was essential to ensure harmony and prevent chaos.

Ka: The Vital Energy

The Ka was seen as the vital energy or life essence of a person. After death, the Ka continued to reside in the tomb and had to be fed by offerings and rituals. The preservation of the body through mummification was crucial for the wellbeing of the Ka in the afterlife.

Ba: The Traveling Spirit

The Ba was considered to represent the spirit and be capable of freely moving between the world of the living and the afterlife. It was often represented as a bird with a human head, symbolizing its ability to travel. The Ba returned to the tomb to reunite with the body (and therefore the Ka) every night.

Osiris: The Judge of the Dead

God of death, resurrection, and the afterlife, Osiris played a central role in Egyptian beliefs about the afterlife. He was the judge of souls, deciding who deserved to join the kingdom of the dead. The myth of Osiris, murdered and then resurrected by Isis, was a fundamental story of regeneration and eternity.

Anubis: The Guide of Soul

God with the head of a jackal, Anubis was the protector of cemeteries and the guide of souls in the afterlife. He supervised mummification and was a key guardian in the soul's journey after death. His role in the ritual of the weighing of the heart, where the heart of the deceased was weighed against the feather of Maat, was crucial to determine the fate of the soul.

The Nile

The Nile, this legendary river, is the backbone of ancient Egypt, a heavenly gift that shaped the civilization itself. In the implacable desert, it winds like a silver snake, bringing life and fertility to its shores. Its waters, fresh and invigorating, contrast with the burning aridity of the surrounding sands, creating an oasis of greenery where life can prosper.

The banks of the Nile are a living picture: verdant fields stretch as far as the eye can see, nourished by the river's life-giving waters. Here, farmers work hard, blessing each flood that enriches their land with fertile silt. Papyrus reeds sway in the breeze, while blossoming lotuses float peacefully, adding a touch of grace to this vibrant landscape.

The Nile is not only a river; it is a deity, a central character in the mythology and everyday life of the Egyptians. It is the creator of all prosperity, the never-ending provider. The ancient Egyptians worshipped, feared, and thanked it for its blessings. The temples and altars along its banks testify to this deep devotion, where priests and worshippers pay homage to this source of life.

The annual floods of the Nile, a phenomenon both dreaded and anticipated, mark the cycle of life in Egypt. These floods, predicted with astronomical precision, transform the landscape, submerging the land and preparing it for the next season of harvest. These floods are moments of celebration, where the community comes together to welcome the new year of fertility. They are the beating heart of agriculture, without which the greatness of Egypt would never have been.

The Nile is also a vital artery for trade and communication. Boats glide on its waters, carrying goods, people, and ideas from one end of the country to the other. It is a link that unites the different regions of Egypt, a path that facilitates the exchange and interaction between the different cultures and peoples.

In literature and art, the Nile is omnipresent, a symbol of generosity and power. It is sung by poets, glorified by artists, and celebrated in countless hymns and prayers. The river is often personified, represented as a generous benefactor or a powerful god, offering its gifts to humanity.

The Nile, with its floods and its beneficent waters, is more than a simple river. It is a living, breathing character, at the heart of ancient Egypt. Its presence has shaped the history, culture, and daily life of this fascinating civilization, leaving an indelible mark on the landscape of human history.

The moon and the sun

The sun and moon, in ancient Egypt, were much more than simple celestial bodies; they were deities, powerful symbols embodying fundamental principles of life, death, and rebirth. The sun, represented by the god Re, was the beating heart of Egyptian mythology, a symbol of power, creation, and regeneration. Each sunrise was a reminder of Re's victory over darkness, symbolizing the promise of a new beginning, hope, and rebirth.

In his daily journey across the sky, Rê was both an ordinary and extraordinary sight. He was the protector, the guide, and the benefactor of humanity, bringing light and warmth, but also a constant reminder of the cosmic order and divine justice. In his solar boat, he traversed the sky, fighting the forces of chaos to bring light to the world every day.

The moon, on the other hand, was governed by several deities, but one of the most notable was Khonsou, God of the moon. Unlike the blazing power of the sun, the moon was more subtle, more mysterious. It was a symbol of change, of cycles and renewal. The moon controlled the tides, influenced emotions and behavior, and was a guide for those who traveled at night.

Khonsou, in Egyptian mythology, was often represented as a young man carrying the moon on his head. He was associated with healing and protection, and his cycles were used to measure time. The moon was also a symbol of femininity, fertility, and birth, reflecting the changing and renewable aspects of life.

Together, the sun and the moon formed a dynamic balance, representing the opposing but complementary forces that govern the world. Their celestial dance was a constant reminder of the cycles of life, death, and rebirth, central themes in Egyptian religion and philosophy. Their influence was visible not only in the skies, but also in the temples, sacred texts, and daily practices of the ancient Egyptians.

The sun and the moon were therefore much more than simple celestial bodies for the Egyptians; they were living symbols of their vision of the world, spiritual guides and protectors, whose cycles and movements dictated the rhythm of life itself.

The Book of the Dead

The Book of the Dead, in ancient Egypt, was an essential guide to the afterlife, a set of sacred texts that served as a spiritual compass for the souls of the dead. It was not a single book, but rather a collection of formulas, prayers, hymns and magical spells, personalized for each individual, intended to ensure the protection, guidance and success of the soul in its journey after death.

The purification of the soul: This chapter included rituals and incantations to purify the soul of the deceased of its past sins. This was a crucial step to prepare the soul to meet the deities of the afterlife and to pass the judgment of Osiris.

The judgments in the afterlife: These texts described the process by which the soul of the deceased was judged. The heart of the deceased, symbol of his conscience and his actions, was weighed against the feather of Maat, representing truth and justice. If the heart was heavier than the feather, the soul was devoured by Ammut, the devourer of souls.

The soul's journey in the world of the dead: These passages narrated the soul's wanderings in the Duat, the realm of the dead, a place full of dangers and obstacles. The spells contained in the Book of the Dead helped the soul navigate this complex world and reach the Hall of Two Truths for the final judgment.

The trials of the soul: The soul had to overcome various trials, face terrifying creatures and cross lakes of fire. Magical formulas were provided to help the soul overcome these challenges.

The offering of offerings: These formulas ensured that the soul of the deceased would receive food and other offerings necessary for its journey into the afterlife.

The magical formulas for protecting the soul: These incantations offered protection against the dangers of the world of the dead, ensuring the safety and well-being of the soul.

The formulas for becoming invisible in the afterlife: These spells allowed the soul to move without being detected by evil forces or enemies.

The formulas for becoming a celestial spirit: These texts helped the soul to become an "akh", a bright spirit capable of living among the gods.

The formulas for reincarnation: Although less common, some formulas evoked the possibility of a rebirth or reincarnation, allowing the soul to return to the world of the living in a new form.

The Book of the Dead was thus a vital tool for the ancient Egyptians, reflecting their complex beliefs about death, the afterlife, and the eternal quest for immortality. Each formula, each chapter, was a step towards eternity, guiding souls through the mysteries of death to the promise of life after death.

Life after death

The conception of life after death in ancient Egypt was both complex and fascinating, reflecting a deep belief in the existence of an afterlife where the soul continued its journey. This belief was rooted in the idea that death was not an end, but rather a transition to another form of existence.

The Continuity of Existence: The ancient Egyptians saw life after death as a natural extension of earthly life. They believed that the essential aspects of their current existence, such as their status, identity, and possessions, could be carried into the afterlife.

The Afterlife Preparation: Mummification, funeral rituals, and richly endowed tombs were essential to ensure a successful and comfortable transition to the afterlife. These practices were supposed to preserve not only the body, but also provide the soul (Ba) and vital spirit (Ka) with everything they needed for their journey and future existence.

The Journey of the Soul: After death, the soul undertook a perilous journey through the Douat (underworld) to reach the Field of Reeds, an idyllic paradise similar to life on earth, but without suffering or illness. This journey was full of challenges, monsters, and judgments.

The Judgment of Osiris: The highlight of this journey was the judgment before Osiris, where the heart of the deceased was weighed against the feather of Maat, symbolizing truth, and justice. This judgment determined if the soul was worthy of immortality.

The Life Beyond: For those who succeeded the judgment, the afterlife offered a peaceful and pleasant existence. Souls could live in houses, cultivate fields and enjoy the pleasures they had known in their earthly life. They could also interact with the gods and other souls.

The Communication with the Living: The Egyptians believed that the dead could communicate with the living. The offerings to the deceased, the prayers and the rituals were ways of maintaining these links and ensuring the well-being of the souls in the hereafter.

Afterlife, in Egyptian imagination, was therefore a mirror of earthly life, but freed from physical constraints and suffering. This profound belief shaped not only their funeral practices, but also their vision of the world, their art, their architecture, and their literature, leaving a rich and unique cultural heritage that continues to captivate the modern world.

The royal blood

The royal bloodline in ancient Egypt was more than just a succession of leaders; it embodied the fusion of the divine with the earthly, a fundamental belief that permeated the very structure of Egyptian society.

Divinity and Kingship: The pharaohs were not only sovereigns; they were perceived as earthly incarnations of the gods, intermediaries between the divinities and the people. This divinization of the pharaoh was at the heart of royal legitimacy and political authority in Egypt.

Transmission of Power: Traditionally, the royal line was passed down from father to son, but Egyptian history is full of examples where women, such as Hatshepsut and Cleopatra, ruled as Pharaohs. These exceptions illustrate the flexibility and adaptability of the Egyptian political structure in the face of dynastic and political necessities.

Royal Family Marriages: In order to preserve the purity of the royal lineage, it was not uncommon for pharaohs to marry members of their own family, such as sisters or half-sisters. These endogamous marriages aimed to maintain the sanctity and purity of the royal blood.

Symbols of Royalty: The royal attributes, such as the Double Crown (Pschent) symbolizing the union of Upper and Lower Egypt, the scepter, and the flail, were powerful symbols of pharaonic sovereignty. These symbols, loaded with religious and political meanings, strengthened the image of the pharaoh as an undisputed divine leader.

Ceremonies and Rituals: The life of the pharaoh was punctuated by ceremonies and rituals that underscored his divine status. These events, often linked to natural and cosmic cycles, such as the floods of the Nile or the movements of the stars, strengthened the link between the pharaoh, nature, and the divine.

The Death and Afterlife: Even in death, the royal lineage maintained its importance. The Pharaoh's tombs, in particular the pyramids, were monuments to the eternal glory of the Pharaohs, ensuring their passage into the afterlife and their divine status for eternity.

The royal bloodline, in ancient Egypt, was therefore a central pillar of society, a symbol of continuity and stability, and a vital link between men, nature, and the divine. This conception of royalty, both human and divine, deeply marked the history and culture of ancient Egypt, leaving a legacy that still fascinates today.

The gods of ancient Egypt were numerous and were associated with various aspects of daily life, nature, religion, and royalty. Here are some of the most important gods of ancient Egypt.

Ra was the sun god of ancient Egypt

He was considered the supreme god of Egypt and was associated with the sun. He was often represented as a man with a falcon's head, with a solar disk on his head. He was considered the creator of the universe and was worshiped as the god of creation, light and life.

Osiris

He was the god of resurrection and the afterlife. He was often represented as a mummified man, with marks of cuts on his body, recalling his death and resurrection. He was considered the guarantor of eternal life for the souls of the dead.

Isis

She was the mother goddess and wife of Osiris. She was considered the goddess of fertility, magic and protection. She was often represented with feathers on her head, symbolizing her protection.

Horu

He was the son of Osiris and Isis and was considered the god of royalty and protection. He was often represented as a falcon or a man with a falcon's head.

Anubis

He was the god of the dead and of embalming. He was often represented as a man with the head of a jackal or a dog. He was considered the guardian of the dead and the protector of graves.

Set

He was the god of violence, of the storm and of war. He was often represented as a man with the head of a ram or a jackal, or as a man with a hooked nose. He was considered the god of evil and was often associated with death and destruction.

Tho

He was the god of wisdom, writing, and knowledge. He was often represented as a man with the head of an ibis or baboon, or as a man with horns and a lunar disk on his head. He was considered the god of knowledge and science.

Aton

He was a solar god of ancient Egypt, who was worshipped during the New Kingdom period, particularly during the reign of Pharaoh Akhenaten. He was considered the supreme god, above all other gods, and was associated with light, life, and creation.

Aton was represented as a solar disk with rays that end in hands holding rings of offerings. He was often associated with hymnic inscriptions that praised his praises and his benefits.

During his reign, Akhenaten imposed monotheism in honor of Aten, and ordered the destruction of temples and statues of other gods, as well as the suppression of priests who served them. He also moved the capital of Egypt from Thebes to Akhetaten (present-day Amarna) to be closer to his god.

Despite this, the worship of Aten did not last in Egypt after the reign of Akhenaten and the traditional gods were restored after his death. However, Akhenaten's religious experience and his worship of the one god had a significant impact on the history of Egypt and influenced theories on monotheism.

DISCOVERY OF THE TOMB

On November 4, 1922, the desert breeze carried with it the murmur of ancestors, as if to guide the steps of Howard Carter and his patron, Lord Carnarvon, towards one of the most extraordinary discoveries in the history of archaeology. After years of relentless research, the Valley of the Kings, this royal cemetery enveloped in mystery, was about to reveal its last secret: the almost intact tomb of a Pharaoh of the 18th Dynasty, Tutankhamun.

The discovery was the result of Carter's tenacious intuition, who, despite the skeptics, had continued to believe that the valley still hid treasures. When the first step was cleared, the excitement was palpable, but it was nothing compared to the emotion that seized the team when the sealed door of the tomb appeared, intact and inviolate for more than 3000 years.

Lord Carnarvon, who had financed the excavations, was present to witness the opening of the tomb. When Carter made a breach in the door, he inserted a candle and, wide-eyed, murmured these now-famous words in response to Carnarvon's impatience: "I see wonderful things."

Inside, the tomb was crammed with an invaluable treasure, a true microcosm of ancient Egypt. Over 5,000 objects were discovered, each telling a story of divinity, power, and eternity. Statues of gilded wooden guardians stood stoically, watching over the young king's rest. Chests overflowing with jewelry and amulets, war chariots ready for the afterlife, ritual beds adorned with divine figures, and canopic jars intended to hold the embalmed pharaoh's organs.

The highlight of the discovery was the sarcophagus of Tutankhamun himself, surrounded by three nested coffins, the last one made of solid gold. On the face of the funeral mask, a portrait of the young king with the nemes, the striped headdress of the pharaohs, and the fake beard, symbols of his divine royalty, was inlaid with lapis lazuli, turquoise, and carnelian, with eyes half-closed in quartz and obsidian that seemed to contemplate immortality.

But beyond the splendor, Carter noticed anomalies. Names erased and replaced on some objects, modified cartridges, indicating that these goods had not been designed for Tutankhamun. Subsequent analysis suggested that some of the treasures had been manufactured for other members of the royalty, perhaps even for Pharaoh Neferneferuaten or Queen Nefertiti, and had been hastily reassigned to Tutankhamun for his journey into the afterlife.

The discovery of Tutankhamun's tomb by Carter and Carnarvon was an event that changed our perception of ancient Egypt forever. It offered an unprecedented glimpse into the life, death, and beliefs of a civilization that continues to fascinate. Tutankhamun's tomb, with its thousands of objects, is a time capsule, a direct link to a distant past, and an inexhaustible source of knowledge and wonder for present and future generations.

ABOUT THE AUTHOR

Claudio Bocchia is a successful entrepreneur in Switzerland. Self-taught at first, then trained in computer development, he creates his first company in 1989, offering digital solutions to SMEs and multinationals. He has formed a team of specialists in digital communication and marketing, photography and video.

For 20 years, Claudio has carried out projects in the banking sector or in multinationals. This expertise coupled with his insatiable need to create, test, deconstruct and reconstruct, makes him evolve with the market. A serial entrepreneur.

Today, Claudio is the head of 3 companies and several brands, some of which are leaders in their market in Switzerland. Passionate about business, computer science and AI, he puts his skills at the service of his clients.

His self-made man journey led him to use his analytical mind to find solutions to the problems businesses are confronted with. He was tasked with finding simple and logical answers to extremely complex problems.

Fascinated by Egyptology, and more specifically by the mysteries of the 18th dynasty, he sought to apply his analytical and logical mind to the history of this fascinating period. By immersing himself in the work of Egyptologists and spending countless hours watching documentaries about ancient Egypt, he has forged a deep understanding of this era. To give life to his ideas and structure them coherently, he chose to collaborate first with Lena Murisier and then with artificial intelligence. This unique approach allowed him to write this book with his original theory, offering unprecedented perspectives on enigmatic historical questions such as:

- Who succeeded Akhenaten?
- How did Tutankhamun die?
- Who is the mother of Tutankhamun?
- Who is Moses?
- Who introduced the monotheistic religions we know today?

Printed in Great Britain
by Amazon

35911263R00086